MW00572234

Cat Tails

Some of My Best Friends are Cats

By Elaine Bailey

Illustrated by Christopher J.G. Bailey

Copyright © by Elaine Bailey 1996

Canadian Cataloguing in Publication Data

Bailey, Elaine Christina, 1945-
  Cat tails

ISBN 0-9680575-0-0

1. Cats-Anecdotes. I. Bailey, Christopher J. G., 1974-
II. Title.
SF445.5B34 1996   636.8   C96-910139-2

Published by Paws Publishing Company
Box 44002
Southcentre Postal Outlet
Calgary, Alberta, Canada T2J 7C5

Cover and text illustrations by Christopher Bailey

First printing May 1996
Second printing January 1997
Third printing June 1997

Printed and bound in Canada by Hands On Graphics
Calgary, Alberta, Canada

Dedication

To the special man in my life who encouraged
me to fulfill a lifetime dream, my gratitude and
deep affection.

TABLE OF CONTENTS

ACKNOWLEDGEMENTS

As is always the case, there are people to thank.

Christopher, for his exceptional drawings;

Sondra, for introducing me to so many of the interesting felines you are about to meet;

Friends who jogged my memory as to various anecdotes or provided new tales.

INTRODUCTION

Ever since I was a small child, I have always had a passion for cats. Over the years, many have co-habited with me. I have never considered ownership of a cat as they are far too regal and elegant. At best, one can be graced by the presence of a feline, but own one, NEVER.

After years of enduring dogs in the family, we finally had an opportunity to share our home with a cat and since then have never been without one or two furry little friends.

Cats are, by virtue of their nature, either loved or hated. There is no middle ground. Those who find a warm, comfortable home in which to live out their existence are indeed fortunate. This doesn't seem to translate into a particular personality trait as was found with the various cats that have occupied our house.

Three such gentlemen cats have been part of the family for years. This is their story, plus a few tales of their friends.....................................

CHAPTER ONE

Minkey Joins The Family

While visiting friends one Sunday afternoon, we were told that their Siamese cat, named Katie, had recently produced a litter of kittens. Being a cat fancier, I immediately asked to see the babies and was totally fascinated by the tiny creatures covered by only a downy coating of fluff. They seemed to consist of enormous ears, long skinny legs and an equally long rope-like tail. The body of the kitten appeared to have been shaven as the exquisite coat of adulthood would not develop for many months yet. They really were not that unusual looking, considering that they were only five weeks old at this time. However, hardly the stately adult Siamese that I had encountered, with their magnificent presence and aloof manner.

One thing I did notice immediately was the different colouring of what little fur the kittens did have. When I questioned the people, I was told that these kittens were, in fact, Blue Point Siamese, which are not nearly as common place as the Chocolate or best known Seal Point Siamese. For such tiny creatures, the babies already had the "points" that defined them as true Siamese. The "points" are that darker toning on the ears, lower legs and paws, the tail and, of course, the face area. The pads of the feet were a soft shade of lilac and looked and felt like velvet. I instantly fell in love with the tiny babies and knew I had to have one to share my life.

What did interest me the most, was the fact that the family had a second adult female Siamese, named Grey, who was just as active in the care of the young kittens as the mother appeared to be. Later on, I was to learn that often more than one female will care for a young litter, especially if there is a problem. In this case, Katie was unwell and having a difficult time nursing the babies so "Auntie Grey" instinctively knew that the little ones needed her help. Both adult cats seemed very concerned for the safety of the kittens and took great pains to put themselves between the children and the babies. They didn't seem to mind when I handled the young ones as if they knew that there was no danger. We soon discovered why they were so protective.

Our hosts had a large family of very undisciplined children. We were told that there had been five babies, but two had already met an untimely end at the hands of the children and the remaining three seemed in peril of the same fate. We watched in horror as four very active small children dragged the defenceless little creatures around the house. Christopher, my son, age five, in true form to his gentle nature and consummate love of animals, couldn't tolerate the misuse of these tiny creatures any longer. Cradling one kitten in his chubby little arms, he came and hid it on the couch beside me with a whispered plea,

"We have to save him, Mommy".

The little guy curled up tightly against me and thus began an enduring relationship between one Blue Point Siamese cat and me that exists to this day!

It has always been my prerogative to name our cats, so there really was very little discussion on the subject. Being of regal ancestry, the young gentleman was to be "Blue Sapphire"—"Blue" for short. However, all that was about to change very quickly.

We have always been great fans of the "PINK PANTHER" series of movies and a favourite scene from one of Peter Seller's classic roles as Inspector Clousseau is as a

Paris policeman on the beat. He has a confrontation with a supposedly blind organ grinder and his monkey, who is in reality the look-out man for a bank robbery. Of course, in true Clousseau style, it gets totally mismanaged, the bad guys get away with Clousseau's help and he finds himself before his superior trying to explain (in his best French dialect) his dealings with the organ grinder and his "minkey".

Upon arriving home with the little Siamese, I was astounded to discover that the little guy was absolutely alive with enough fleas to start a flea circus and spares left over! Since we already lived with a rather aged tabby, I wasn't keen to have a flea epidemic on my hands, so the poor little chap was immediately subjected to a flea bath. As cats are less than thrilled with water at the best of times, this baptismal was not greeted with great enthusiasm. Amid tiny protests and sharp little claws, I finally got the job done and had a huge heated bath towel all ready in which to roll the baby so he wouldn't catch a chill.

After a cuddle and a rubdown with the towel still wapped snugly around him, his motor started up and was soon going full blast. For such a tiny bit of kitten, he had a rich throaty purr. I uncovered him and there was the most woe-begotten little face with ears far too big and his tiny bit of fur plastered to his body. The final indignity was when I held him up to inspect for any tell-tale lingering fleas and his long rope-like tail wrapped around my arm. At that precise moment, Les looked over and laughing at the poor cat, said,

"Hey, Lady, where did you get the 'minkey'?"

Well, there it was. Out went "Blue Sapphire", in came "Minkey". Never one to allow anyone the last word, I insisted on tacking "San" onto the name of such a lovely Siamese gentleman, so he became "Minkey San". "San" is an oriental title of respect and rather in keeping with his background. This was to come back to haunt me later on.

I discovered early on that Minkey had an undying affection for wool blankets and would knead and purr while happily sucking on a wool blanket. There has always been such a blanket on my bed and every night from the time that Minkey came to join us as a five week old kitten, he has slept tightly curled up beside me, happily sucking and purring his way into sleep. It can be a somewhat noisy ritual some nights, but I find when I am away from home, I miss the sounds and they never bother, but rather soothe me as much as they do Minkey. Even as he nears his 17th year, he continues to need his "blankey" every night and simply will not settle down, but continues to pace and fuss until he is indulged. Over the years, there have been several "blankeys" which have to be duly broken in and there is quite a routine to this. First the new blanket is inspected and ignored while wild protests are heard throughout the house. Finally, he will grudgingly accept the offending blankey, but only after he has stomped around on it, rolled on it to give it his scent and finally, he licks an area until it is a soggy mess. Thus satisfied, he settles in to suck and knead, purring contentedly to let me know that all is forgiven and the new blankey is acceptable.

Traits in cats are very individual. Minkey demonstrated his special personality early on. He loved and still loves to be warm all the time. No doubt it is a result of his ancestral background of coming from a warm climate, but he loves heat. He has always has a very thin coat of sleek fur which doesn't seem to thicken greatly in cold weather. He will follow the sun from room to room all day. On days when the sun fails to shine, he wanders aimlessly from room to room complaining bitterly that he can't find his sunny spots. It gets so annoying sometimes, that I find myself apologising that the sun can't get through the cloud cover. This does seem to placate him, as he will then wander off to find another heat source. He always needs heat around him and often I will enter a room in the dead of winter and comment on how cold the room is, only to find Minkey firmly and squarely spread on the heat vent, totally blocking any escape of a fragment of heat. How he can lay there by the hour and not totally scorch his belly has remained a mystery to me for many years.

When Minkey was only a few months old, I had a rather serious ski accident, which resulted in my being laid up in bed with a series of huge casts for several months. Mother came to stay and help out, but she and Minkey had never met and they had a few things to sort out, such as who ran the recovery room.

The Red Cross kindly lent us a blanket raise for the bed. This was a wonderful device that allowed blankets to be draped over the leg without pressure. It also provided a delightful little cosy house for Minkey and he took up permanent residence at the foot of the bed. In his little "tent", cosy and warm, he slept the days away, only venturing forth for a quick visit to the food bowl or the litter box. For him, this was an ideal arrangement—here was warmth provided by his adopted mom (me) and a secure place for him.

Unfortunately, Mother had other ideas as I required foot massages to encourage circulation that was critical to the healing process. This meant that on a regular basis, the blanket tent had to be moved. Every time Mother would reach to move it, out would come an elegant long grey paw, claws extended like tiny needles and with rapier quick speed, would slash out at her. She finally nicknamed him "The Brat" and, until she passed away, Minkey received his annual Christmas gift addressed "To Minkey, The Brat, from Grandma". They finally resolved their differences and Mother became one of Minkey's favourite "people". Whenever she came to visit, Minkey appeared out of nowhere at the sound of her voice and greeted her with great affection. An honour reserved only for his closest friends.

Since I was incapacitated for many months, various family members came to help out. This was also the time when Minkey was still a very young gent who spent all of his time with me and the bond was strongly formed during those months as I could give him all the attention he longed for and missed with having been taken from his natural mother at such an early age. It should be noted here, that very shortly after Minkey came to live with us, his mother died and Minkey was the only member of his family to survive. This only made him more special to me. During my recuperation time, my sister was spending time with us and one morning, she came to tell me a wonderful story amid much laughter. It seemed that Minkey had taken to tormenting our elderly tabby, Misty, who simply wanted to be left alone. She had not reconciled to this young upstart joining the family and she longed for the days of quiet solitude. After suffering in silence, Misty had finally had enough. She was quietly sunning herself, enjoying the view from the low set window and Minkey chose that time to continually pounce on her tail as it slowly glided back and forth. To be fair, she gave him due warning with a series of throaty growls, which he chose to ignore. The story went that Misty allowed him to venture closer and closer until finally with lightening quick speed, she reached back and smacked him so hard that he was knocked completely across the room. He hit the refrigerator and lay in a heap, dazed for a few seconds, then quickly beat a hasty retreat to the safety of my bed. That ended his days of tormenting Misty. She continued to gaze out the window and totally ignored him. One can only imagine her sense of satisfaction at putting the young one firmly in his place.

It was about this time that Minkey started to feel his spirit and after racing around the house in a frantic imaginary chase, decided to climb the drapes to the ceiling. It was definitely time for him to make the trip to the vet to be "fixed". As the spay/neuter clinic was on route to Les's work, it fell to him to deliver the cat on the fateful day. All the arrangements had been made, the cat was in the cage having fasted overnight and off they went. What I failed to realise was that other than the trip home to live with us, Minkey had never set a paw out of the house, much less made a journey in the car of some duration. The trip was a wild ride through early morning rush hour traffic with a howling Siamese who tried to claw and chew his way out of the cage.

By the time they reached the clinic, it was looking more

and more like this could be a one way trip if things didn't improve and quickly. At this point, we were still calling the cat "Minkey San". Unfortunately, things slowly deteriorated as the cat decided that he didn't like the whole idea of the clinic or the smells and refused to be removed from the cage. Since the attendant was in another room, Les attempted unsuccessfully to get the cat out and in the process, made a few references as to Minkey's oriental background which were not necessarily complimentary. He had just made a rather pointed reference complete with a few profanities, when the cat decided to comply with his wishes and the attendant appeared. Les was so intent upon the squirming cat that when the attendant asked for the cat's name, he replied that it was "Minkey San" and then came face to face with the attendant, an oriental gentleman! From that day on, Minkey lost his grand title of "San" and has been know ever since as Minkey.

CHAPTER TWO

Minkey's Tricks and Traits

When Minkey was about five years old, I decided to purchase a waterbed. Needless to say, I had major concerns as I had heard horror stories of how water beds and cats claws simply were not compatible and should be avoided at all cost. However, since my ski accident I had been through a series of reconstructive surgeries which left me suffering with arthritis and the prospect of sleeping on an eternally warm mattress, not unlike a giant hot water bottle, seemed a lovely idea. After a good deal of consultation with various salespersons, I was convinced that with a heavy padding developed especially with sharp little claws in mind, I wouldn't wake up one night to a rather wet environment. With this in mind, I went ahead with the arrangement.

The existing bed was dismantled and moved to another room which sent Minkey into a state of shock as he hates any kind of upheaval so disappeared to the farthest reach of the house to avoid the uproar. In due course, the waterbed was installed, filled with warm water and ready to use. By this time, Minkey's cat curiosity had got the better of him, or he missed his blankey, and he ventured upstairs. Upon seeing what he assumed was his regular bed back in place, he came flying across the room and took a mighty leap into the centre of the bed. If ever a cat could have a shocked look , it was a picture to behold. He stood frozen in position as if attempting to get his sea legs and gave the appearance of a drunken sailor after a night on shore leave. He seemed to get the feel of it eventually and began to slowly bounce up and down as the water lazily ebbed and flowed under him.

Then the reality of it all hit him. Not only was this fun, but if he laid down, it was lovely and WARM. That did it. This was too good to be true. He set up a howl that only a demanding Siamese can make and when his now famous "blankey" was made into a nice bed, he proceeded to curl up and go to sleep. There he has slept ever since on average of twenty hours a day!!!! I maintain that humans are only allowed the use of the bed at Minkey's discretion and certainly never in his space.

All cats love high places and most enjoy the company of humans. One could never presume to own a cat as they are truly free spirits, but cats will pick the person they prefer to spend their time around. Such was the case with Minkey. When I was home, he liked to be in the same room with me and being rather social, he felt that if we were in the same room, it was only right that I should talk to him or at least pay attention to him, even if he decided to fall asleep. A favourite spot for him was on the kitchen fridge, as it had a great vantage point to watch all the activities, but certainly saved on the tail getting stepped upon. I would become involved in a project and completely forget that he was in the room until I went near enough at which point, he would extend an elegant grey arm and gently tap me on the head. Needless to say, more that one egg was broken as the shock of a paw tapping my head startled me and interrupted my train of thought.

Because Minkey loved high places and his favourite was the fridge top (always nice and warm in the kitchen) he spent a lot of time there. When the children were small, I was always scolding them for not closing the fridge door properly as I would walk into the kitchen and find the door wide open. Imagine my embarrassment when Mother informed me that she had watched Minkey sleeping on the fridge. He woke up, stood up, gracefully stretched, arched his back into a lovely Hallowe'en cat pose and sprung off the end of the top, thus catching the door with his back claws and dislodging it. He then strolled out of the kitchen, totally unconcerned as the fridge door slowly glided open! The children were incredibly smug to think that the "golden cat" Minkey was actually capable of doing anything wrong and more important, getting caught.

Minkey liked to join me when I did the laundry as then he could lay on top of the warm clothes dryer and ultimately burrow into the still warm clothes as they were piled into the basket, fresh from the hot dryer. In the laundry room, there was a beam on the ceiling and attached to the beam was a cross bar about six inches wide. By jumping onto the deep freeze, Minkey could spring up to the cross bar and perch while I did the laundry. If no warm clothes came out of the dryer, he would ascend to his perch and watch all the activities from there. One day as he sat there, I looked up and said,

"So, can you hang ten?"

Imagine my shock when he dropped his fore paws over the bar and hung by his hindquarters!!!! This was unbelievable, or just a chance happening. I left the room with a load of laundry and he promptly jumped down to follow me. I continued with house work and eventually laundry time came again so off we went to the laundry room. He immediately jumped up on the cross bar and sat watching me. This can't happen twice, I thought, but why not give it a try.

"Hang ten, Mink," I said and was amazed as he promptly dropped the front paws and hung there. From then on, he always did his trick for me and when we moved to another house, he was quite upset to find that all the beams were built in and his days of "hanging ten" came to an end.

Minkey's love of high places sometimes got him into more difficulty than he planned on. A new challenge presented itself when he was introduced to his first Christmas tree. Great care had been taken by the family to chose just the right tree, it had been securely anchored in a pail of moist sand and the family was ready to trim it. After several hours of painstaking care and preparation, the tree was a delight to behold and having admired the lights and decorations, the family went off to bed. All was quiet until the wee hours of the morning, when there was a sickening crash. We rushed out to find the tree tipped over onto the carpet and wet sand spread far and wide. Still clinging to the top most branch of the tree was one absolutely terrified little grey Siamese cat. I had to pry his claws out of the branch and from that day on, he never bothered any Christmas tree again.

Over the years, Minkey developed quite a repertoire of neat tricks that he would do if the mood moved him or he wanted an extra scratch on the tummy. When he was quite young, he discovered that by tucking his head between his front paws, he could actually turn a complete summersalt. He would glide over as if in slow motion and then stretch out to his full extent in order to receive the full effect of a tummy scratch and great verbal compliments on his stunning ability. As he gets older, the old bones don't respond quite as well, but since he still loves to get a body rub, he finds that if he balances himself against a piece of furniture, he can still achieve a very passable roll and get the desired rub and praise. If the summersalt is a little off centre, he manages to look as if he really planned it that way and loudly demands additional praise.

Another trick that Minkey developed, came much later in his life. This was very surprising as most cats will not do tricks of any kind as it is just too demeaning and best left to the lower life forms, such as dogs. So for Minkey to learn a trick at an advanced age was rare, indeed. It happened that another kitten joined the family and this little guy could actually sit up on his haunches and beg. It was truly a sight to see. I was so fascinated by his balance, that I started to reward him with special kitty treats. Minkey watched all of this attention being lavished on the young feline and finally decided he wasn't going to take second place to a bit of fluffy kitten. The next time I went to get the treats, I turned around to find not one, but two cats proudly balanced on their haunches waiting for praise and a treat. Never one to be outdone, Minkey had added a verbal note by giving me one of his long whining howls and demanding additional rubs. From then on, it became a contest between the two gents to see who could maintain the pose for the longest duration and still gobble down the goodies.

Although not given to begging as a general rule for Minkey, there is one exception and that is when I open a package of bacon and the first frying smell assails his little nose. He will be fast asleep in the bedroom and the minute that the bacon starts to fry, he is under my feet, howling as if he hasn't had a decent meal in a week. As the plate of bacon is carried to the table, he continues to make a terrible noise and tries to trip me. Then he sits and stares at me until I relent and offer him a tiny morsel. He accepts it daintily between his front teeth and devours it. Then the routine is repeated until he has satisfied his taste buds, at which point he loses interest until I decide to fry bacon again.

In many ways, some of Minkey's traits are not unlike that of a child as he craves vast amounts of affection and attention. One of his favourite games is to play hide and seek. He will pretend to be totally bored and pay no attention to what I am doing, at which point, I will quietly go into another room and hide. Then he will start to howl and search until he finds me, only to give me a look that clearly says, "I knew where you were all the time". This, of course, is followed by great demands for rubs and the game starts again.

This game will also extend to making the bed as Minkey will jump up on the bed, I will cover him with the linen and then wonder aloud where Minkey has gone. He will howl loudly and laying on his back, kick the blankets to let me know where he is and that he wants some attention and rubs. It has never occurred to me until now, how odd it would look to someone walking into the situation to see a grown woman playing hide and seek with a rather aging Siamese, but I guess that is what true friendship is all about.

He has given me many years of enjoyment and companionship.

Minkey has always prided himself on being a fastidiously clean gentleman feline. This has led to some rather unusual character traits. Whenever he used the litter box, he would pile all of the litter into a huge mound in the middle of the box and in the process, spray a good deal of it onto the surrounding floor area. Finally in desperation, I purchased a "Kitty Potty". This is a litter box with a lid and entrance way, which solved the problem of litter spread everywhere. However, it also created somewhat of a hollow sound. Now every time Minkey uses the litter, he will proceed to scoop the litter into a neat pile. This scratching and scraping will go on for a considerable length of time and can become quite irritating.

Some years ago, my brother came to visit and he was given the guest room right next door to where the litter box was kept. It is only fair to note here that he would not be considered a great cat lover and at best, tolerates my cats. In the middle of the night, Minkey found the need to use the box and having finished, went into his routine of scraping, scratching and building his mound of litter. Awakened from a deep sleep, my brother was treated to, in his words, an eternity of scraping.

As he described it the next morning over breakfast, when he did go to investigate, it was the most incredible sight he had ever seen. He found all of the litter neatly piled in the centre of the box and Minkey admiring his handiwork. My brother said that the cross-eyed Siamese fool reminded him of an Egyptian excavating to build a pyramid. From then on, that guest room was always known as the "Pyramid Room" and whenever he arrived for a visit, there was a note on the door welcoming him to the "Pyramid Room" and it was signed by Minkey.

CHAPTER THREE

Minkey; the Three Fanged cat

When Minkey was about twelve, he broke off one of his front teeth, which I referred to as his fang. Not knowing how or when it happened, I was very concerned about problems later on and was trying to decide how to proceed. I had no idea how it may affect his health or eating ability. I had noticed the tooth was missing just as I was leaving the house to get groceries and my mind was still very much on what course of action I should take as I pushed the cart through the store. As luck would have it, I chanced to meet a good friend who also happened to be a dentist. There in the middle of the grocery store aisle, I proceeded to bend his ear with my worries regarding the cat. Knowing that I had a passion for my cats and tended to baby them, he heard me out and assured me that there wasn't a great deal to be concerned about.

Imagine my surprise when the doorbell rang later in the evening and there stood the dentist and his wife. He carried a very good bottle of vintage wine and his wife had a lovely bouquet of flowers. Peter announced that he was making a house call to consult with the patient and had not really come to see us. After a very thorough examination, he announced that the fang had broken off cleanly at the gum line. He assured me that Minkey was in no pain at the moment, but that he may develop problems in the future so I should keep a close watch on it. We then proceeded to empty the bottle of vintage wine and admire the flowers.

Some three years later, I arrived home one evening to find Minkey in terrible pain and actually frothing at the mouth. Since he never went outdoors, I couldn't imagine what the problem could be until I went to touch him. It was the only time that Minkey actually growled at me. I realised that he was in need of medical attention immediately and called the vet. Although it was after hours, the vet took my concern seriously and arranged to meet me at the clinic at once. I have often said a silent prayer of thanks to his caring and compassion as his quick response actually saved Minkey's life that night.

When I arrived at the vet's office, Minkey was definitely in distress and wouldn't allow anyone to touch him, let alone do a proper examination. The vet did determine that the gum was terribly infected and the root of the broken fang was still firmly imbedded in the gum. He didn't seem very hopeful given Minkey's age and the degree of infection; however, he gave Minkey a massive injection of antibiotic and I was told that if he made it through the night, he may be able to survive surgery once the infection was under control.

Totally devastated, I prepared for the worst possible scenario, which would be to say good-bye to my much loved friend. Once home, I made him as comfortable as possible with his special blankey on the water bed and settled down to spend a very restless night and listen to his laboured breathing until the medication took effect. Eventually, I must have dosed off and was awakened to a terrible sound of thundering feet. I went to investigate and stood in stunned silence as I watched Minkey chasing the younger cat, Nathan around the house and actually rolling and romping with Nathan.............. obviously, the medication was working. Needless to say, I felt tears of joy running down my face.

After a week of pumping Minkey full of antibiotics, we were off to see the vet yet again. I think that the vet was rather surprised to see Minkey as he hadn't been very positive in his original diagnoses. This time he cautioned me that although we had got past the first hurdle, the surgery to remove the remainder of the tooth in the gum still lay ahead and he would also need all of his teeth cleaned which meant anaesthetic for a period of time. Minkey's kidneys were not functioning as well as a young cat's would and the stress on his heart could be too much for him. I wanted to wait at the clinic but was advised to go home and they would call when they had news. I went home to wait and pace the floor. The indication was that it would be several hours before I heard anything, so when the phone rang about an hour and a half later, I was filled with dread. A very cheery voice announced the vet, who informed me that Minkey, the old gent, was doing just fine, the surgery was a success and he would be waiting for me to pick him up later in the day!

When I went to collect Minkey, I found him rather tired, curled up on his blankey in a heated enclosure, looking every bit the invalid, with a look that clearly stated, "It's about time you came to rescue me". Minkey always has the uncanny ability to appear aloof even in the most undignified situations so I feel compelled to apologise for any discomfort he may be having, even when I knew for certain that he had received the very best care and the vet was responsible for saving his life. I was overjoyed to have my little friend home again.

The vet informed me that with the incredible loving care and affection that Minkey received, he could live well into his twenties. A wonderful piece of news for me, but I'm not certain that the rest of the family shared my enthusiasm. This may be reflected in the fact that he was dubbed, "Minkey, the old three toothed cat" by certain members of the family.

CHAPTER FOUR

Travels with Minkey and Friends

Because of the nature of work, we were required to move often and this created some unique problems when transporting cats. On one occasion, we had to move to another city about a hundred and fifty miles away. Keeping in mind that at this point, the only car trips that Minkey had ever made were when he came to live with us and the disastrous trip to get "fixed". Not only that, but we now had three cats, who all had to be transported at the same time and none of them were fond of car travel. After discussing it at length with the vet, it was decided that all three cats would endure the journey better if they had a tranquilliser. The day arrived for the road trip, the travel cages were lined up and all three cats were ready to "hit the road". I pried open each little mouth and as they clawed and protested, I managed to pop in the pills.

Safely secured in their cages, we waited for the pills to take effect. All went quiet after an hour, so we settled the cages gently in the back seat and started off through the city traffic. Aside from the occasional slurred meow, things were going well or so we thought. Not too many miles down the road, the choir began to sing. It was not unlike listening to a reunion of "good ole boys" after a few drinks. First one cat would start and since it seemed like such a good idea, the second joined in, followed by the third. There is nothing quite as terrible as the sound of three drugged felines in cages confined to the back seat of a very small car on a very hot summer day. Since the "singing" seemed to take on a life of it's own, Minkey decided that he would add a rhythm section and put an elegant arm out through the wire door of the cage and hooked his claws firmly into the back of the front seat. Thus anchored, he proceeded to pound on the seat at just mid-back level. I had no idea of his strength, no doubt born of his fear and the drugs. It was, without a doubt, the longest car journey I have ever endured.

Arriving at our destination, we found that a minor earthquake had dislodged the ceiling plaster in our temporary accommodation and we were forced to seek lodging in a motel. Unfortunately, there was a huge convention in progress and the only available motel came to be known in the family as the '"roach motel". I was a little concerned when I saw the machine that took quarters so the bed would vibrate! The bathroom sink was not connected to the drainage pipe, so when the sink was emptied, it just ran onto the floor. There was no stopper for the bathtub, but one look at the interior of the tub made us all opt for showers, and quick ones at that. These were not exactly the conditions the family was familiar with, but we decided to make do for one night. No one had said anything about pets and we certainly didn't ask.

All three cages were deposited in the room and I set up the litter box and a fresh bowl of water. Then the cages were opened and the cats were allowed the run of the area. The younger cats strolled out in rather good shape. I soon discovered why one was so alert. As I shook out his blanket to rearrange his sleeping area, the pill I had so cleverly given him fell on the floor. He had spit it out and this explained the serenading we had suffered through.

Poor Minkey had not faired so well. He had felt the full effect of the tranquilliser and was staggering around the room, totally disorientated. He would only stop howling if I carried him around the room like a baby. Keeping in mind that Minkey is a 16 pound cat, it is a rather awesome sight to see such a large cat being carried about like an infant. As I was trying to get him calmed down, the chamber maid knocked on the door with extra bedding. She started to tell me that pets were not allowed, but Minkey chose that moment to start his unearthly howling and his eyes rolled back into his head, leaving only the filmy white showing. I can only imagine how I looked with a sixteen pound drugged Siamese draped over my shoulder and in no mood to listen to any nonsense after spending several hours in a car with screaming cats. No doubt the frightened girl thought that the cat was possessed by a demon as she turned and ran, never to come near the room again while we stayed there.

Minkey would try to make an attempt to stand up and simply could not find his centre of gravity. Any attempt to lay down proved equally devastating for him as he would try to do the mandatory three circles before settling down and end up falling off the bed. I spent most of the night retrieving him from the floor where he continued to fall each time he would attempt to get comfortable. He continued to wail in a plaintive voice that was as disorientated as he was. Needles to say, none of us got much sleep, but that really didn't matter as the vibrating bed was about as comfortable as sleeping on a pile of rocks. I kept thinking that the following day, we had to meet the moving van and get our belongings into the new house. We were meant to spend a second night in the "roach motel"; however, the first thing I asked the movers to set up were the beds and the following night we slept happily amid packing boxes in our own beds.

Once moved into our new home, all of the cats were allowed free access to roam and discover their new surroundings. Minkey disappeared and was discovered the following day, holed up in the rafters of the basement. I could only think that he had enough of the upheaval and was looking for a secure place to regroup and recover from the trip and perhaps to sleep off the effects of the drugs.

When Minkey was twelve, he made what would be his last major trip, which was completely across country by air. I have learned that for long distance travel, airlifting is by far the best way for cats to move. This time, I would be travelling with him and he would be very comfortable in his deluxe carpeted travelling cage, complete with blankey to snuggle down in for protection. The tranquilliser was administered and we were off to the airport.

The trip went smoothly and when I went to retrieve him from the cargo dock, I was very concerned as he would not respond to my calling his name. Eventually, he did move enough and I saw that his ear was damaged. He had obviously caught it in the slats of the cage and there was a notched area that had been bleeding. I simply couldn't understand what could have disturbed him so much. He was absolutely terrified and seemed frozen, totally unable to move. At this moment, a young man arrived looking for his pet and was delighted when an enormous cage was unloaded. He opened the door and out leapt a Great Dane.

Upon investigation, I discovered that poor Minkey had endured a four hour flight with his rather small cage perched atop the dog's much larger cage. Apparently, the young fellow didn't feel it was necessary to prepare the dog for travel by sedating him and told me that the dog was always hoarse from barking after every trip. I can only imagine poor Minkey's terror as not only does he not even go outdoors, he had never encountered a dog and certainly never at such close range for so long. I made a promise to Minkey, then and there, that in future, the only trip he would ever make would be his visits to the vet!

CHAPTER FIVE

Cat facts: Minkey Style

As has been mentioned before, Minkey loves total attention and will demand it on his terms at any time the mood moves him. He loves to stretch out on his back to his considerable full length and present his "arm pits" for a scratch. He actually stretches his front paws over his head as far as he can, his body will arch and his head will be thrown back to reveal his neck and chin. There he lays and demands by raspy howls, that he wants a full body rub and scratch. To stop too soon incurs a resounding ear shattering howl of protest and he will then follow me around trying to trip me up in order to continue. One must never decide for a cat when they want attention. Any self respecting cat makes that decision and nothing will change their mind.

Most cats are very communal and live comfortably in a group environment. From experience, I have discovered that new additions to the group are much better tolerated if introduced at a very early age. I make it a practise to handle the new member of the family in order to get my scent on his coat. Then the little one is allowed to wander and explore the new surroundings. It is quite amazing to watch as the older cats will first sniff out the new arrival, hiss and growl as if to give their "pecking order" in the pride and then allow the youngster to check out the litter box and food tray. Amazingly enough, the older cats will actually allow the baby the first chance at the food bowl and then take turns to eat in order that everyone gets some food. There doesn't seem to be any special requirement for male or female as all adult cats will care for each other equally.

It is not unusual to find two of the adult male cats grooming each other and they will then curl up and sleep quite peacefully together for hours. It would appear that the over-riding factor is the well being of the community and in Minkey's case, the extra body heat never hurts. Over the years, I think that Minkey, as senior member of the community , has accepted me as part of his "pride". I have awakened on more than one occasion to find him grooming my hair and he will continue until he is satisfied that it is done properly. Having finished, he will then curl up against my head and purring contentedly, drift off to sleep.

There is definitely an order in the group and every so often, one of the younger members will decide to challenge this. For some reason known only to a bunch of felines, this usually takes place at about three o'clock in the morning and is accompanied by the most incredible noise. They always decide to do this settling of accounts either on the bed or right beside it. It starts with low throaty growls and then proceeds to a few hisses. As things start to warm up, they increase the volume and proceed to shift for position, which can be a little unnerving as the only thing between sharp claws and the body is a thin layer of blankets. At this point, I suggest that they take their dispute elsewhere. Never one to be distracted, Minkey will defend his ground to the last and has been known to literally throw another cat off the bed by kicking at him with very powerful back legs.

The second phase seems to involve a great chase around the house. For such small animals, they make a thunderous sound of galloping paws that sound like a herd of stampeding elephants. It will culminate in an awesome tackle that any football player would be proud of, and amid flying fur and howls of protest from the "under-cat", the dispute will be settled and Minkey will stomp off, tail held high, to find his blankey and curl up for a sleep. All will go quiet and in the morning, I will find the odd clump of fur, but more importantly, nine times out of ten, the combatants will be snuggled up in a ball together, fast asleep.

For reasons known only to cats, they have a strange fascination with wood. Wood in any shape or form is considered fair game upon which to sharpen claws. The fact that it may be an antique piece of furniture that has been in the family for generations cuts no ice with a cat in need of a good clawing post. To purchase a spiffy new manufactured post is a terrible waste of money as no self respecting cat would ever consider using so convenient a device.

Over the years, one can actually develop a reasonably good ear for furniture being clawed at the other end of the house, and in some cases, even recognise the culprit involved. Minkey has left his trade mark on several pieces of good furniture, but his favourite are the dining room chairs. I will hear his very distinctive rapid clawing and yell for him to stop. Moments later, he will meander into the room and I have always maintained that if he had pockets in which to put his paws and could whistle, he would do both things then! The only give-away is that the other cats look at him as they always do when one of them is guilty of the crime. No such thing as honour among thieves. It's every cat for himself.

Many times I have heard stories about how animals warn of impending danger with astounding accuracy. Minkey displayed this ability only once. We lived in a part of the country that occasionally had earthquakes. None were as dramatic as those suffered by Californians, so we were totally unprepared for the quake. I had retired for the night and had just settled into a deep sleep when Minkey began an unearthly howling and proceeded to literally run up and down my body. He clawed at the covers on the bed and continued to howl until I was fully awake. I became aware of the fact that all of the cats were behaving very strangely, making incredible noise and running frantically from one family member to another. Suddenly, I heard what sounded like a locomotive train coming from the east at a phenomenal speed. The sound and quake hit the house and reverberated through the entire structure as it passed on to the west. There was an eerie silence as the cats became mute with fear and then the after shock hit. It all happened very quickly and then was gone. I lay in bed trying to gather my wits and then went to check on the children. Amazingly, both had slept through the entire episode!!! We sustained only minimal damage and the children were terribly disappointed to think that they had missed the excitement. Interestingly enough, my daughter now lives in Southern California and takes the quakes in stride as do most people that I have met from that area.

Can cats tell time? Any cat that has ever lived with me certainly knows when to expect things to happen. Feeding time at the zoo is always in the morning and they will allow a certain amount of leeway for the occasional lay-in, but if it goes past eleven a.m., all bets are off and some one is always designated to walk on me until I am sufficiently awake to hear the complaints. It is slightly disconcerting to be brought to total consciousness by five hungry felines. They stare balefully at me, taking turns to voice their displeasure and stomp all over the bed. Forget about a cup of coffee before feeding them as they simply will not allow it. Try to read the paper and they magically know the very paragraph being read and will sit on that particular article. It is far simpler to just feed the beasties and proceed with the routine after that.

As I start toward the stairs to prepare the food, five cats with tails held straight up create an advance guard. They all have their own bowls and feeding area so proceed to gather like staving children, each one voicing his or her demand for goodies. Like children, the younger ones will bat at each other, pushing and shoving for the best position in hopes that they will get their food bowl first. Minkey has to be fed on top of the dryer in order to get a fair shot at his food. As he has got older, he eats very slowly and unless feeding time is supervised, the other cats will finish their food and push him out before he has a chance to get a fair share. Once they have all had a feeding time at their own bowl, they proceed to move around and check out each others left-overs which really amuses me, because they all get exactly the same food, but somehow, it must taste a little better coming from the other cat's place!

How Minkey hates to see a suitcase. Whenever I plan a trip and the suitcase comes out of storage, Minkey goes into "pout" mode. He refuses to talk to me, turning his back when I try to give him any love and glares balefully at the offending suitcase. Once the actual packing starts, he kicks into high gear and "Operation Obstruction" goes into effect. I will pack a layer of clothes and go to collect more things. When I return, one of two things will have happened. Either all of the clothes will be pulled out of the suitcase or the second scenario is that he simply plants himself in the middle of the clothes and gives me a look that clearly states, "If you must go somewhere, I'm going with you"! To move him out only upsets him so I end up packing layer upon layer as he shifts to allow clothes to be snugly packed around him.

When the final garments are packed, I will leave the lid ajar to allow for the last minute things to be added. On more than one occasion, I have been startled to lift the lid and find Minkey curled up on my clothes, fast asleep. The end result is that when I arrive at my destination, there are little reminders of Minkey in the form of shed fur and creased clothes. When I return home, he reluctantly allows me to greet him and only relaxes when the hated suitcase is totally unpacked and he escorts me to safely store it away again.

Bedtime for Minkey is a ritual. When bedtime rolls around, Minkey will appear wherever I happen to be and simply sit down regally beside me and proceed to stare. I'm convinced that if he wore a watch, he would keep checking the time and tap his paw on the crystal, just to remind me. Once I've started up the stairs to bed, he throws himself down in front of me, tripping me and loudly demanding to be carried up to bed. He happily purrs and emits delighted little howls in an incredibly raspy voice as I pick him up and carry him over my shoulder like a small baby. Once in the bedroom, I always lay him down gently on his blankey and he settles in to suck and purr his way into another night of contented sleep.

I had no idea of the number of human-like qualities that cats will develop over a period of time until something happens to draw attention to it. One night, I was awakened from a deep sleep and couldn't quite identify the noise I heard or where it was coming from, only that it was very near and loud. Not wanting to disturb the household by turning on lights, I lay quietly listening and suddenly, the reality of it hit me. Minkey was snoring!!! It was a rather cold night and he had crawled right under the blankets with me and was curled up in a warm ball, deeply asleep and snoring his little heart out. Whoever said that cats have it rough, has never met Minkey.

As Minkey grows into his twilight years, he spends more time sleeping and dozing in the sun spots or on his beloved water bed, curled up on blankey. He never passes up a warm lap to curl up on, accepts all the attention given to him and looks for more and is always there when I'm feeling very low or extremely happy. One couldn't ask for a better or more loyal friend and I would be lost without him.

He has taken to joining me while I write his story and has a large chair next to me in which he sleeps curled up on his blankey, naturally! Snoring.

CHAPTER SIX

Enter Charles

Everybody should have a cat like Charles in their lives. Like all our cats, Charles came to us from very sad beginnings and we took him in to give him the love and security that all cats crave and deserve.

My daughter, Sondra shares my passion for cats and over the years has brought several home to share our lives. Charles was no exception. One weekend, she had been invited by a friend to attend a country fair and while there, had seen a farmer's booth set up that was giving away kittens. She was thrilled and rushed over to choose one, only to discover they were all spoken for already. The farmer said that he had also given some away to people who had left the fair grounds. She continued to enjoy the fair, but the kittens remained in her mind. It would never have occurred to her that another cat in the family wouldn't be acceptable as any cat she ever brought home was always welcomed.

As she was returning to the friend's car, her attention was drawn to a group of young boys who seemed to be having a game of toss football. She went closer and was appalled to find the boys were using a kitten as the football. It should be noted here, that Sondra is a very small built person and a feather weight. She was so angry at the misuse of such a tiny creature that she pushed her way into the middle of the group of big boys, walked over to the chap holding the pathetic kitten, doubled up her fist and shook it in his face, demanding, "give me that cat"! As her friend

described it later, the boy was so taken aback, that he simply handed over the cat without a word. Tucking the kitten inside her coat, she turned on her heels and marched out of the group.

Once home, we discovered that his back had been damaged and his tail was broken, but we were determined to keep him and took great care to treat him gently until he healed. As always, I insisted on naming him and since he was white with a black saddle shape on his back, he had a somewhat regal air about him and I named him "Charles". Little did I know that he would become thrilled with mud and many times Minkey would give him prolonged baths just to clean him up. Before long, his name had been downgraded to "Chuck" and he is affectionately known as "Chuckie Cheese" in the family. He certainly has never been overly bright, but is by far the most loveable cat we have ever had live with us.

Because of his injuries, Minkey seemed to sense that the little one needed to be dealt with gently and never tried to bully him. By the same token, Chuckie never really cared about being the leader of the pride and is happy just being a cat doing his own thing. The two of them have always co-habited very well together and rarely ever have a cross word. Also, at this time, Minkey was much younger and more ready to accept new additions to the family. As he grew older, his tolerance level was not as accepting of more felines. Perhaps he feels that it divides the affection too many ways.

Of all our cats, Chuck has always been the most sociable. He loves to be around people and is very chatty with everyone. He will walk into a room, tail held high and verbalise away, going from one person to the next by way of greeting and never misses anyone. Of course, this works to his advantage as well as he gets extra rubs and pats, not to mention the occasional treat thrown into the bargain. His favourite form of receiving affection is to have both of his sides slapped vigorously. This reduces him to a lump of jelly and he will actually fall over on his side as the side slapping increases. Too much, however, will result in him getting totally carried away and he will start to claw and bite in excitement. Knowing just how much attention to give him becomes critical to the hands.

As mentioned before, all cats have their own character traits and Chuckie is no exception. He absolutely loves mud. Not unlike a small boy who would rather walk through the puddle than around it, Chuck is thrilled to find a nice wet patch of ground. Not only will he walk through it several times, just to get the feel of it, but if the mood moves him, he will even lay down in it and have a nap! Later on, he will arrive at the door wanting to be allowed in and one look at his telltale formerly white coat sends me off for a wet towel. Then begins the game of trying to catch him as he comes through the door. After so many years, he knows what the towel means and has learned to be very foxy about leaping through the door and across the clean floor before I can catch him.

It was discovered very early on that Chuck had another passion also associated with water. He loves spending time in the bathroom. If anyone goes into the bathroom, they can be guaranteed of having a visitor join them. He will sit in the sink, plaintively pleading to have the tap turned on and will then stick his head right under the running water as he refreshes himself. He has also been known to get an unexpected bath as he will hear water running and gallop into the bathroom, up onto the tub edge, lose his footing on the metal and find himself in the water. There is something to be said for closing the bathroom door before running a bath unless one really enjoys taking a bath amid floating Chuckie fur.

Chuck will amble into the bathroom whenever he knows someone is there, demand a pat by leaning against a leg and then jump up onto the vanity and gaze at the poor, unsuspecting soul. Of course, Chuck always feels that a person is somewhat of a captive audience while in the bathroom so he takes this opportunity to let one know how much he REALLY likes them. This will include a gentle tap on the shoulder and keeping in mind that Chuck doesn't always remember to keep his claws in, this can prove somewhat painful. When there is a quick reminder that claws are not acceptable, he always manages to look very concerned, waits about ten seconds and then taps the shoulder again. This will continue until he is acknowledged and then he likes to do cheek-to-cheek. He will actually put his face out in line with the "guest" and patiently wait for the person to put his face beside Chuckie's. Chuckie then purrs delightedly and leans in to make better contact. If prepared, this can be rather a touching moment; however, for most people, it is just very unnerving! As one guest wrote in the guest book after visiting:

"Had a wonderful dinner and visit, but watch out for the cat in the bathroom!"

For all that Chuck loves mud and the water in the bathroom, he has no great love for being caught in the rain. He will go determinedly to the door demanding to be allowed out and no amount of trying to explain to him that it is raining seems to penetrate his brain. Off he gallops into the stormy weather and before long, there is a plaintive howling at the door to indicate that he wants back in the house. Not one to be subtle, he stomps around complaining about being left out in the rain and then rubs against everyone until I have to get a nice soft towel and he stands quite regally as I give him a good towelling down to warm him up and get his coat nice and dry. He then struts off to have a sleep.

CHAPTER SEVEN

Chuckie's Friends

Chuck has always been considered to be a bit of a thug in the cat population of the family. Because he is a rather large gent, he stomps around making a lot of noise, but is in reality, a true pussy cat. One house we lived in had a storage shed in the back yard. It had been suspected that there was a family of skunks residing under the shed, but as they are rather docile night creatures, no effort was made to move them out.

Across the street from the house, there was a crop of bushes about six feet high. On many occasions, I watched various cats, tails held high, march across to those bushes and disappear into the hedge. I could only conclude that it was the local hangout for the feline population when they wanted to get away from the "rat race", as they all seemed to have a grand time and upon returning home, would sleep for hours. Chuck's rather sociable nature took over as one evening, I glanced out the window and to my amazement, strolling across the street and directly into the bush line was Papa skunk, Mama skunk, Baby skunk and bringing up the rear, tail held straight up was a very familiar white and black cat, namely, Chuck! One by one, they plunked into the bushes and disappeared.

My first thought was to call to him, but fearing the skunks might become frightened and spray, I kept quiet. Instead, I went to check on the supply of tomato juice which I felt certain would be needed when the skunks discovered

Chuck was following them. Several hours later, his voice could be heard at the door and I was prepared for a rather smelly entrance so was ready to grab him. Imagine my surprise when he strolled in, totally unconcerned, with no hint of skunk odour. I could only conclude that his great personality had saved him and he continued to socialise with the skunk family for the time we lived in that area....................

It was some two years later that once again we were on the move and this one was right across the country. This meant that the cats had to be airlifted about 3000 miles and they had to be prepared for a four hour flight. The night previous to leaving, the cats had to fast and would be given medication to help them make the journey in comfort. I had been very careful to explain all of this to the children and cautioned them not to let the cats get out of the house. In the evening, Christopher, who was now in his teens, came home having said good-bye to his friends and feeling rather sad, didn't pay attention as he entered the house.

Just the opportunity that Chuck has been waiting for as he leapt out the door and made for the now famous bushes. I ordered Christopher to retrieve the cat and off he went in pursuit of the escapee. A good deal of time elapsed, then I heard the front door open and rushed to help with the struggling cat. It was then that I caught a whiff of Chuck. He absolutely reeked of skunk spray. If one has never been introduced to an animal that has been sprayed by a skunk, one cannot even imagine the smell. It will actually bring tears to the eyes and cause one to gag.

I was so angry that I told Christopher to take the cat to the garage and I went to fetch the necessary ingredients. A vet had told me that the best way to remove the smell was to douse the cat in tomato juice and work in well as the spray actually penetrates the skin. That done and washed off, an application of lemon juice is next, followed by a bath in Extract of Strawberry shampoo. The process is repeated and hopefully that eliminates any remaining smell. Poor Chuckie looked so dejected by the time we had finished. Sadly, in bathing him, all of his own scent was removed and as cats know each other by scent, he became an outcast in his own family. The other guys growled and hissed at him, not allowing him to venture near them. It was only later that I couldn't help but wonder if he had gone to say good-bye to his pals, the skunk family, and they had given him a bit of a send-off for being such a good friend!

At the new residence, there was a very high fence with a nice ledge that the cats loved to stroll along. At one point, the next door neighbour had a rather yappy, small dog that Chuck obviously didn't like. He took great delight in sitting on the ledge and just staring at the dog, which sent the dog into fits of yapping and leaping at the fence. I always maintained that if Chuck could have stuck his tongue out at the dog, he would have done so with great delight. The neighbour would eventually come to investigate at which point, Chuck would quickly jump off the fence into his own yard where he couldn't be seen and smugly listen as the dog got a scolding for making noise and marking the fence with his nails.

There have been times when this guerrilla warfare didn't actually work to Chuck's advantage. There were a number of squirrels in the area and they, too, liked the ledge as a strolling place. The neighbour on the other side also owned a dog, but this one was a large black Labrador who really hated cats. One day, a squirrel decided to take a little walk at the same time as Chuck. The squirrel was totally unaware of the cat, so Chuck decided to stock the beastie. After all, from his point of view, this was nothing more than a tree rat! Along the ledge went the squirrel followed by Chuck and soon they were both around the corner and within sight of the dog.

The squirrel came to the end of the fence and jumped down out of sight, followed closely by Chuck, who was so engrossed in the squirrel that he failed to realise that he was about to descend into enemy territory. Chuck leapt off the fence, there was vicious snarling and barking and almost instantly, Chuck reappeared back over the fence in one mighty bound. He must have been so terrified that he actually cleared the seven foot fence and landed in the back yard. It appeared as if he had jumped into a trampoline on the other side as he reappeared so quickly and with such force. He hit the ground on the dead run and didn't stop until he was safely on the deck. This did not stop his fence walking, but he has now developed a very good idea of where his property line ends and the dog's begins.

CHAPTER EIGHT

Traps

Chuckie seems to have his share of adventures and is constantly getting caught in traps. At one place where we lived, the yard backed onto a sound berm, beyond which, there was a farmer's field. These sound berms were built to reduce the traffic noise from a main highway, but they also became a haven for various wildlife that liked to burrow. This particular area was rather heavily populated with groundhogs. They certainly are not vicious creatures; however, they can do considerable damage to gardens as they tend to like to take a taste out of each growing vegetable and leave the rest to rot. Now, I don't mind sharing with wild life, but it got to the point where they were totally destroying the garden. In desperation, I finally called the local SPCA, who kindly leant me a trap. Success came quickly as the trap was full the following day. A trip was made into the countryside, where the groundhog was released.

Knowing that groundhogs live in a group, I decided it would be a great idea to try again, in case he had a wife and family, so the trap was reset. Bedtime came and there was no sign of Chuck. Calling and whistling got no response, so he was going to spend the night outdoors. In the morning, I went to check the trap and there sat Chuck inside the box, looking very sad faced and more than a little frightened. As I opened the cage, he literally cleared my head in his hurry to escape.

Like Chuck, I didn't know when to stop with the trap. Having reset the trap, I waited to see if I would be successful in catching another groundhog. The following day, the children went to check the trap and came running in, pleading with me to keep the cute kitty that was now caught. My first thought, was that now I had trapped a neighbour's cat and would have to explain. No such luck! When I went to investigate, I was appalled to find a skunk placidly nibbling on a piece of carrot. I beat a hasty retreat to the house and called the SPCA to come and collect their trap. They advised me to just drop the trap off at the shelter and were concerned as to why I was reluctant to do that. When I informed them that it was occupied, the operator started to explain that I only needed to take the trap out in the country and release the animal. When I told her that it was occupied by a black beastie with a white strip down it's back, there was a slight pause. I was assured the someone would be there as quickly as possible.

The children and cats watched in fascination as the gent from the SPCA arrived in his van. He took a rubberised sheet from the van and slowly and quietly made his way to where the trap was set up at the far end of the garden. He gently approached the trap, draped the sheet over the entire area and strolled off with the trap, the skunk inside still munching on his lunch. That was the end of my trapping days!!!!!!!!!!!

One would think that Chuck would have learned his lesson, but as Chuck is not very clever, he continued to meet with disaster. Upon moving to a new location, I discovered that the city had a cat by-law which stated that all cats must be kept on a leash or indoors. Not necessarily a bad by-law, just ill conceived as cat are not like dogs, who are willing to be tied up. Also if one can train a kitten to leash, they generally do well, but to tell a ten year old cat that he suddenly has to be indoors all the time or tethered, just doesn't work. Any attempt to keep the cats indoors when they are accustomed to going out, resulted in howling, lost sleep for everyone and refusal to use the litter box. The idea of tethering the cats outside soon proved futile as they either became hopelessly tangled up in the lines or simply slipped out of the harness and were off anyway. In desperation, they were allowed to move freely about and I soon found that they rarely ventured very far from home.

The part of the by-law that I did find offensive was that any citizen was authorized to obtain a regulation live trap from the city and could actually lure cats into being trapped. They, then, took the animals to the local shelter where it remanded for three days and if not claimed, was destroyed. To recover a pet involved a substantial fine plus boarding fees. Since many people were unable to afford these hefty rates, their pets became forfeit and met with an untimely and tragic end.

The neighbour who owned the Labrador didn't see it quite like that. Chuck loves his food and never misses meal time, so I became concerned when he failed to return from a stroll one night. However, it was a warm night, so thought he had decided to spend the time on the prowl. By the next afternoon, I was really alarmed and insisted we call the animal control. A description was given over the phone and after checking, were told that no white and black tabby had been turned in to them. A little later, the phone rang and the animal shelter said they had received a cat from our area of the city, but that it was a brown tabby. The lady was requested to go and see if he responded to his name, "Chuck". She returned moments later, with positive identification. Chuck was definitely there and sitting on Death Row.

Les was despatched to spring the convict and when he arrived at the shelter, he went to identify the cat and there sat Chuck, facing the wall with his back to the viewing area, pouting. As his name was called, he rushed over to greet this familiar face and was thus rescued from death row. He must have got the idea, as we haven't had any repeats of traps since then.

As Chuckie's fine was being paid, the animal control officer commented, "I'm so glad you came for your pet. So many people can't afford to and it really is a tragedy."

Sadly, this is altogether too true, and many beautiful animals are destroyed by unfeeling people driven by foolish laws and narrow minded attitudes. Perhaps that is why we are so compelled to give outcasts such loving warm surroundings.

CHAPTER NINE

Chuckie Habits

Like all cats, Chuck likes his creature comforts and will spend his days indoors should the winter blast descend upon us. He can usually handle being inside for about three days and then he becomes 'hut happy' and demands to be allowed out. Keeping in mind that this is a self-imposed confinement, he is offered the opportunity to venture forth on a regular basis. When he simply can't stand it another minute, he stands at the door howling to be allowed out. As the cold air hits him, he quickly backs away and rushes to another door, hoping for a more favourable climate on the other side of the house. Like a high diver making a death defying leap, Chuck will charge to the door, take a breath and leap out into the Arctic blast. Once the cold actually penetrates his coat, he comes to a full stop, gives a baleful look and does a 180 degree turn as he retreats to heat.

Chuck likes to play a game called "Wrong side of the door". This game consists of Chuck finding someone who is gullible enough to let him in and out of the house a dozen times a day! He indicates that he wants to go outside and will fuss until he is let out. Minutes later, he is howling to be allowed in again. This game will continue until the person gets fed up and refuses to play any more. Chuck will try one last time and just to get rid of him, the door will be opened. As the sliding door is opened, Chuck will make a mighty leap to go out, not realising that another door still has to be opened and he will crash into the glass of the second door. Thrown back, he struggles to his feet, gives a drop dead look and stomps off, refusing to exit by that way for the remainder of the day. It is pointless to try to explain to him that he simply has to slow down.

The deck at the back of the house was the easiest access route for the cats to get to the large enclosed backyard so was used regularly. Below the deck, five feet down at ground level was a concrete patio area. Unfortunately, over a period of time, the floor of the deck became unsafe and required major reconstruction. Ripping up the floor proved to be a real task and after several backbreaking hours, only a small portion had been removed leaving a hole right at the top of the steps. Barricades were set up for safety overnight. As a result, the cats were re-routed out the front door while the repairs took place; however, Chuck refused to co-oper-ate when it was time to come in for the night. He stead-fastly insisted that he would only use the deck entrance and any attempt to change his mind just sent him scurrying off, making it impossible to catch him. In the wee hours of the morning, his constant meowing and howling awakened me and being only half-awake, I stumbled to the deck entrance, opened the door and completely forgetting about the gapping hole in the floor of the deck, urgently called for him, in order to stop his noise.

Out of the night there appeared a streak of white fur and as the realization of the gaping hole registered on my addled brain, Chuckie hit the stairs at top speed. Nothing was going to stop him getting in the house by HIS door. Before I could even yell, he was up the steps and I watched in horror as his little body disappeared head first into the hole. It was like watching a disaster in slow motion as he tumbled over the edge, the pink bottoms of his feet fading from view. There was a dull thud and total silence. I began to call his name and was rewarded with a single very soft meow. As I gingerly prepared to made an attempt to cross the remaining deck, a little white face appeared at the top of the stairs. He scoped the deck as if he was wearing radar and then carefully and very slowly picked his way across to safety. Other than being winded, he appeared none the worse for wear, but he did agree to use the other door until the new floor was installed and only after testing it, one paw at a time, was he convinced that all was well and he returned to using that exit.

Chuck has developed what can only be described as a very annoying habit. When he wants to get someone's attention, his first line of attack is to become very verbal and simply will not shut up. If one is trying to concentrate, this can become very annoying and Chuck is told in no uncertain terms to move along and be quiet. Having failed in this attempt, he moves on to phase two, which is to make several passes as close to one's leg as he can and actually caress the leg with his tail and at the same time emit a throaty sound like 'brrrrrut'. If this ploy doesn't get the desired attention, he brings out the big guns, which means he simply climbs up into the person's lap, walks up the front of them and stares straight into their face. When least expecting it, he will start to purr contentedly and gently butt foreheads and nibble on the nose. This can be quite a nice form of communication except when he has had fish for lunch, in which case, I wouldn't recommend it!!!!!!!!!!!!!!

Catnip. Just the mention of the name makes any self respecting cat's mouth start to water. It is especially good for the cats when they have to spend long periods of time confined to the house as it gets them moving and they then get much needed exercise. For years, I have allowed the cats small amounts of it, but Chuck is the only cat I have ever seen who reacts to it so wildly. From experience, I first spread large amounts of newspaper all over the kitchen floor. Then a small amount of catnip is sprinkled into the centre of the paper.

Minkey is the first to explore and will eat some, get a faraway look in his eyes and curl up for a nap. So much for the exercise theory. Nathan rolls around in it, gets his heavy fur coat covered, becomes mildly active and quickly loses interest. Then Chuckie wanders over, gets a sniff of it and the fun begins. He absolutely goes wild. He rolls around like a mad thing, spreading the catnip all over the room. He lays on his back, howls and kicks his feet in the air, which is quite a sight with his fat belly! He tries to crawl under the paper and slithers around the floor on his tummy. The most disgusting part comes next as he will start to drool and before long, the paper has been reduced to a soggy mess in places. Finally, he engages in a frantic gallop around the house at full speed, making his way from room to room as he charges into furniture and bounces off, never slowing his pace.

By this time, it is always a good idea to clean up the kitchen floor as Chuck will gallop through, spreading paper and whatever catnip is left all over the room. Totally exhausted, he will finally calm down and find a nice sun patch in which to sleep it off. The kids maintain that catnip is the best "high" for Chuck so we only give it to him about three times a year.

Chuck has never been a great hunter and prefers to get his daily intake of food from a nice clean bowl. However, for a period of time, our home backed onto a bird sanctuary and this became more than he could bear. One day, we discovered him in the back yard playing with a tiny baby Starling. Having caught the little bird, he had absolutely no idea of what to do with it and was simply playing with it. He seemed rather bewildered when Sondra took the half dead bit of feathers from him and gave him a severe scolding. She then took the bird into the house and spent the next twelve hours caring for it. She made a secure little nest and prepared a soft mixture of pabulum with a tiny dose of antibiotics and fed the bird with a tooth pick every hour. We felt that if the little one made it through the night, it would have a chance. The following day, the bird seemed to have regained some strength and we delivered him to the SPCA. There, a lady was waiting to take the little one and care for it until it was old enough to be released into the wild.

After a great deal of discussion, it was decided that

Chuck would have to wear a collar and bell. He was fitted with the collar and allowed outdoors, only to return a short time later, minus the offending collar. Another collar was obtained, a bell attached to it and off he went again. This scenario was repeated a number of times, until in desperation, I finally gave up. He obviously felt he had made his point as he never brought home any more birds nor was he subjected to the indignity of a collar and bell again.

Chuckie has been both a delight and a pain in the neck over the years, but a more loving and devoted friend one couldn't ask for and we would all be poorer if he hadn't been rescued by Sondra and joined the family.

CHAPTER TEN

There's a Rat in the House

As the years passed, various cats came to live with us. The children would try to slip in the odd stray, but I insisted that the population maximum was three. More than that number simply became overwhelming to care for and to give proper attention. We were at the required quota as I left for a holiday, leaving the family at home. Nothing was said about an addition to the group on the ride home from the airport, so I was totally unprepared for the bedraggled fluff ball that scurried out from under a table as I entered the house. Without thinking, I exclaimed,

"There's a rat in the house!" and then realised what a really stupid comment that was, considering the three cats who lived there.

After some coaxing, the kitten was retrieved from under the furniture and I came face to face with my first Maine Coon Cat. Here was a tiny ball of tangled fur, pointed ears with fur growing out of them in a sweeping fashion and paws that gave the illusion of being webbed with fur. I reached over to pat him and was rewarded with a mighty "chomp" from tiny needle sharp teeth. This was definitely not acceptable and clearly this kitten wouldn't fit into our group of older gents.

The kitten cowered back, expecting to be slapped, but instead, I cradled him in my arms and slowly, his little motor began to softly purr. Here, clearly, was an abused

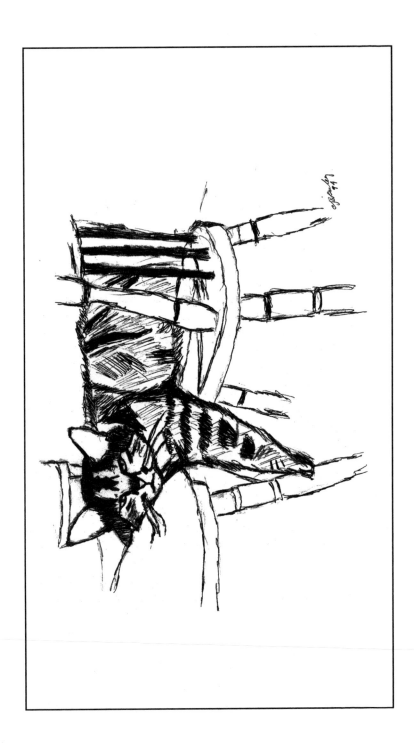

little guy. It seemed that a friend of Sondra's had received the kitten as a gift; however, the family already had very expensive pure-bred Oriental cats. Naturally, the kitten wanted to play, but hadn't learned how to control his tiny claws yet. He just wanted to play with the big guys and had inflicted an injury on one of the adult cats. This had resulted in the kitten being declawed, a practise of which I disapprove, and the claw beds had not healed properly. It was evident that he was in considerable pain. It also left the little guy totally defenceless, so he had resorted to biting to protect himself.

I also learned that he was kept in the bathroom and only allowed out when the young girl was home. As a result, he had no real interplay with other felines and wasn't really certain of his own identity. The children had been trying to find a good home for him, but I knew that he had already found that home! I was told that when Sondra first brought him to the house, she put him down in the front hallway and he promptly christened it with his scent. For one so tiny, it was a clear indicator that he had chosen where he wanted to live and who could argue with a cat's decision!

The kitten had been named "Cougar" by the young girl, but I wasn't too impressed with that name so after some consideration, he was re-named "Nathan". No real reason why I chose that name other than he had the air of a natty cat and Nathan seemed appropriate. To this day, Christopher still insists on calling him "Cougar" and at every opportunity, tells me what a really cool name it is and how it suits the cat. At times, I have to admit that I agree as Nathan alias "Cougar" definitely has a wild side. He will often lay flat on the floor, making his eyes mere slits and wait to ambush unsuspecting felines simply minding their own business!

As always, the in-house crowd had to give Nathan a full going-over and let him know where he stood in the pecking order, which was way down at the bottom. After the usual sniffing, growling, stomping and hissing, he was left to explore his new surroundings and cautiously inspected all the important places such as the food and water bowls, and most important of all, the litter box! Within a matter of two days, he was one of the crowd and sharing the communal sleeping areas.

Cats use body language to express how they feel and the most expressive part of their anatomy is the tail. One thing that we noticed immediately was that, unlike all cats, Nathan would not carry his tail held high. He would scurry around the house with his tail dropped so low, that sometimes it was almost dragging on the floor. At first, I feared that like his paws, he had an injury; however, a complete examination revealed nothing. After some research on the matter, I came to the conclusion that he really didn't feel that great about himself and was thus intimidated. Assuming that a little positive action was necessary, the family decided to shower him with praise and encourage him to hold his tail up. Thus began "Operation Hoopy Tail".

Every time Nathan would walk, or rather slink past anyone, he would get a warm greeting and be told, "Hoopy tail, Nathan". It seemed to work, because before long, he was attempting to hold his tail aloft. Now, when Nathan enters a room, he struts in carrying the most elegantly plumed, gently swaying tail held straight up! You've come a long way, baby!

CHAPTER ELEVEN

Nathan and the Great Outdoors

As time went by, Nathan decided that he would like to become an outdoor cat, if the temperature was warm and no wind was blowing. Nathan simply can not abide having wind blow his fur coat. He must have extremely sensitive skin and he will only allow very gentle strokes to be administered to his little pelt and any slip that results in his fur being pushed the wrong way will immediately suffer a rather sharp "chomp" from his lightening quick teeth. He is the consummate example of "never rubbing a cat's fur the wrong way".

With his new-found joy of the outdoors, he developed a new game. If he went out one door, it seemed only right that he should return by another entrance. I sometimes wonder if cats are, perhaps, just a little superstitious as rarely will they use the same door to go out and return. This situation proved to be something of a problem as I would let him out the front door and proceed with whatever project I was involved in, often completely forgetting that he had gone for a stroll. In the beginning, he would wait patiently for me to appear at the door at some point to play doorman for him. However, one day the wind started to pick up as a storm neared and I was totally unaware of this, but Nathan's ruffled fur told him that it definitely was time to be indoors.

I suddenly became aware of an insistent banging on

the back screen and went to investigate. There was a cross bar on the sliding screen door about four feet off the ground and there hung Nathan by his front paws as he frantically kicked on the screen with his back legs. He clung steadfastly to the cross bar until I opened the glass sliding doors and only jumped down as I moved the screen door. From then on, he always announced his intention of wanting in by noisily and insistently banging on the door while holding on for dear life to that cross bar.

At this particular residence, the next door neighbour also had a young cat and Nathan and Rover soon became fast friends. This was most unusual as cats who co-habit will do so in harmony for the most part, but rarely will they tolerate a strange cat within their territory. I can only attribute this friendship to the fact that both Nathan and Rover were kittens when they discovered each other and because their property lines joined, they decided to enjoy each other's company. It was really cute to watch as they would actually come to call on each other to go out and play.

I would be in the kitchen and hear a plaintive little meow, at which point, Nathan would appear out of nowhere and demand to be allowed out. There would sit Rover and the two would rub noses, sniff each other and rush off down the stairs to chase each other through the tall grass. Sometimes, I would just stand and watch them as they enjoyed the sunshine, totally carefree and I was reminded of two small boys playing in the summer. My neighbour told me that Nathan also called on Rover and even took to hanging on her screen door cross bar and kicking it to get her attention. They often played in her house on rainy days as Rover wasn't made to feel overly welcome by the other cats in our house.

Nathan wasn't always so generous with his friendship and when we moved from that area, he became very territorial, which was probably due to his maturing and need to protect. One such territorial incident happened some years later. As has been mentioned before, Charles was always considered to be the bully in the family, but that simply was not the case. He was just so big that no other cat thought to cross him. In the new area, there was a rather nasty large tom cat, who really was a bully. He seemed to dominate the entire neighbourhood with his quarrelsome nature. He reminded the family very much of the cartoon cat one sees, who has a patch over one eye and a rather dirty shabby bandage bound around his crooked tail. We had no idea what name this rogue went by, so he was dubbed 'Lurch' after the character of a horror movie.

Charles and Nathan enjoyed spending a warm afternoon sunning themselves on the back deck and were quite content to take an occasional lazy walk around the large enclosed back yard. They were protected from attacking dogs, nasty little boys with sticks or rocks and had a great advantage in that if they wanted to go outside the yard, there was a nifty little hole just big enough to squeeze through. This took them into the next yard, just to see a different part of the world and do a little exploring. What was really critical to remember is that cats don't like to be put in a corner and they have a difficult time if they have to back up as they are forced to turn away from an enemy, thus putting them at a disadvantage.

'Lurch' had become more and more aggressive as time went by and even took to sitting on our deck banister, peering in the kitchen window and spitting on it. Charles had obviously had a run-in with him on occasion, as Charles returned home with the odd battle wound which would be cleaned up and soon healed. One day, 'Lurch' decided to chase Charles right up onto the deck and cornered him. My attention was drawn to the howling from both inside and out as Charles begged to be let in, while Minkey and Nathan watched out the window and tried frantically to get at the bully who dared to attack their brother. I rushed to rescue Charles and had to actually use a broom to chase off the vicious cat. I became very concerned for the safety of both cats who went outdoors, but mostly for Nathan as he had no claws and wouldn't be able to defend himself as well. I need not have worried.

A few days later, there was the most unholy cater-wauling going on in the back yard. When I ran to save the cats from what I knew was another 'Lurch' attack, I was amazed to find Nathan, the smallest of all the cats, fur puffed out until every hair stood on end to give him volume, howling at the top of his little lungs as he slowly and defiantly backed 'Lurch' down the stairs of the deck, across the full expanse of the back yard, through the hole under the fence and then followed him, still howling like a demon from hell. Nathan actually backed 'Lurch' into the next yard at which point the former bully turned and ran for home. What was most amusing about the entire battle was that Charles sat perched on the banister of the deck and watched in total fascination as the rather one sided show unfolded. He wore a look that clearly said, "So that's how you do it"! 'Lurch' has never set a paw in our yard again and by all accounts has stopped tormenting the other cats in the neighbourhood. I can't help but think that Nathan's motto must be one of "I might be small, but I sure know how to bluff".

When Nathan first started to go outdoors, he really wasn't aware of how quickly the weather could change in the latter part of the year. We live in a climate that can be quite unforgiving and we take great care to insure that the cats are logged in and out of the house at all times of the year. In the winter, it is especially important as they can freeze the pads on their paws very quickly on the snow and ice. One evening, Nathan managed to slip out of the house as guests were leaving and made a dash for freedom. I knew that a winter storm was approaching and was very worried about finding him before it hit. Repeated calling and searching proved fruitless as a cat who doesn't want to be found can actually be within arm's length and not let anyone know where they are.

The storm hit with violent winds and blowing snow that piled up around the house. The temperature dropped to an alarming low and I haunted the windows and doors, hoping to see my fluffy little friend making his way home. Several hours passed and I had given up hope of him surviving the intense cold and snow, because he was, after all, an indoor cat unless the weather was fine. As the storm raged on, I busied myself around the house and eventually went to the garage for something. As I passed the small door in the garage, I thought I heard a faint crying and after struggling with the partially frozen door, managed to get it open.

There was the tiniest ball of fur tightly rolled up with only his eyes and nose showing. He was so cold that he couldn't even unroll his body and I scooped him up, forced the door closed and ran with him, calling to the children to bring me a warm blanket. He had ice crystals formed all over his coat and his eyelashes were caked with ice. He somehow had manage to find his way back to the house, but unfortunately, was at the only door that was seldom, if ever, used. What stroke of fate made me go to the garage on that stormy winter night, I'll never know, but obviously, someone out there was watching over Nathan that night. From that time on, Nathan and I have become fast friends and we seem to have a special understanding. He has also developed a healthy respect for winter and only ventures forth if it is an especially mild day. Otherwise, he is content to toast his paws in the warmth of the house.

CHAPTER TWELVE

Nathan Fables

Maine Coon cats have a wonderfully silken coat that is very thick and sleek. They are a hardy breed and some say that they originally came to North America on sailing ships and were let run wild. Like all good stories, there may or may not be truth to it. They do, however, have an interesting colouring to them that gives the impression of a racoon, especially around the eyes, as they appear to be wearing the mask and have the stripped marking in the coat. For the most part, they can tolerate the cold and build up a very thick coat when it is cold. This creates something of a problem as the spring arrives and Nathan finds he is overheating. He would not allow me to brush him as his skin is so sensitive, although over the years, I tried various brushes.

Instead of accepting my help, he preferred to roll around on the concrete sidewalk in an attempt to rid himself of the excess fur which drove him wild as the days grew warmer and warmer. Needless to say, this tactic resulted in his coat becoming a tangled mass of fur. Fortunately, as summer came on, he usually managed to shed the mess and other than collecting vast amounts of fur from furniture and carpets, I dealt with it. However, one year, he really outdid himself and ended up with the most incredible tangled mess. After discussing it with the vet, he suggested a bath and using cream rinse to break up the fur. Two baths later, several chomp marks in my hand and totally frustrated, I resorted to a pair of scissors and gave a cat his one and only hair cut. When I was finished, poor Nathan looked as if he had been attacked by moths.

He must have been embarrassed beyond belief as he became quite nasty and wouldn't allow anyone to touch him. The tangled fur was matted right to the skin so that in some places, he actually had bald patches as a result of my clipping him. In desperation, I took him to the vet who put him to sleep, spent a great deal of time gently combing his fur into its lustrous sheen and presented me with a bill that brought a lump to my throat. He suggested I invest in a good brush and use it on Nathan on a regular basis. Eventually Nathan's coat all grew back in and he forgave me and actually allowed me to groom him for a period of time. I can only guess that he found the entire experience as frustrating and upsetting as I did. Unfortunately, the intensely cold weather created a thick coat the following winter and by late spring, it had become a tangled mess as he resorted to rolling around on the grass and concrete in a attempt to shed the excess.

Finally, I located a delightful lady who clipped poodles, but was willing to help rid Nathan of his massive coat. So now each year, Nathan is given a pill to slow him down and arming myself with a pair of thick gloves, we take a trip across town and as I carefully hold him, he receives a clipping from neck to tail during which I can hear him softly purring. Once finished, he looks rather odd with a huge mane around his face and a long skinny body ending in a huge plumed tail, but he must feel much better as he is much happier and actually demands lots of stroking.

Nathan totally fascinated me with his uncanny ability to sit up and beg. This bit of showmanship led to many special treats being passed his way and even Minkey was caught up in the game and learned how to balance quite well. However, Nathan has always been the master of the game and can out-sit Minkey. Anytime he does his trick for me, he is allowed only three treats and then is told he gets no more. He always tries for an extra few and will do what has come to be known as "cutesy cat". He knows that the treats are kept on top of the fridge and will actually walk into the kitchen, look at me, then at the goody can, back at me and whip into his little pose, paws tucked neatly against his chest and thus perched, remain completely still for as long as it takes for my will power to cave in. The only thing he moves are his eyes which dart back and forth between the goodies and my face. Best con artist in the family as it always works!

Cats and dogs simply do not mix. A statement that most people would agree with; however, like all things, there is the exception to this rule. At least as far as Nathan is concerned, he makes his own rules. Friends of ours have a toy Pomeranian who is about the size of a guinea pig. She is mostly fur and very little else and is very appropriately named 'Peanut". For some strange reason, known only to Nathan, he took a fancy to her. I suspect it is partly because she is so small, being even smaller than him, and he doesn't feel threatened, but he quite fancies her. It is quite cute to see as Peanut's "daddy" will arrive with her tucked inside his jacket and I'll call to Nathan that Peanut has arrived. He rushes in and they proceed to play like old friends. What really is amazing is that Minkey and Charles will come to investigate, see Peanut and turn tail and run to hide, not venturing forth until Peanut has been gone for a considerable length of time.

On occasion, our friends come to visit and for various reasons, Peanut is left at home. Nathan will look for his little buddy and when he realises that she isn't with the family this time, will climb up beside her owner and purring contentedly, will sleep there for the entire evening. We have decided that Nathan can smell Peanut's scent and it is comforting to him.

CHAPTER THIRTEEN

Nathan's Sleeping Habits

Without a doubt, Nathan's most endearing quality if his self appointed role as official host to all house guests. It matters not who the house guest is, as long as they occupy the guest bedroom, he feels it is his job to make them feel comfortable. As soon as the guest arrives, he will escort them down the hall to the guest room. He then hops up on the bed and waits expectantly while they open and unpack the luggage. I'm not certain if he holds out a vague hope for presents, or if he is just curious as to the contents of the bags. Should any clothing be left laying about, he feels it is his chosen job to take a nice nap on the garment. This is especially true with any dark clothes, as not only does he put his scent on things, he can shed a few pounds of his massive coat all over everything.

When bedtime arrives, he is happily waiting for the guest to settle down for the night and will snuggle in against their leg, purring contentedly and sleep the entire night away with them. There is only one rule for house guests and that is to please not close the door as Nathan becomes very irate if shut out of the guest room and will bang on the door making a terrible row until he is allowed in. It is simply easier to comply than be awakened by his indignant noise in the middle of the night.

My oldest friend in the world comes to stay a couple of times a year and fully expects Nathan to be her companion while visiting me. She came to visit once in the dead of winter and I asked if she would prefer flannel or cotton sheets.

Without a moments hesitation, she replied, "Which does Nathan prefer?" I'm told that the two of them slept very comfortable on the cotton sheets with an extra blanket that Nathan is especially fond of using.

When no house guests are visiting, Nathan divides his time among the various members of the family, going from bed to bed. I am so accustomed to having cats sleep with me, that I never feel them arrive or depart. Recently, I began to have problems with my back and would awake in the morning with a terrible pain in the lower back area. A visit to the doctor did not uncover any reason for the pain and it was suggested that perhaps the bed was the reason or the fact that I sleep on my stomach. His diagnosis was closer to the mark the he realised.

I soon discovered what was causing the discomfort as I woke one morning to find Nathan curled up fast asleep in the hollow of my back. When he sleeps, he becomes dead weight so I was enduring his fourteen pounds centred squarely on me. Not only does he insist on sleeping on me, but as I turn, he moves to maintain his place and thus resembles a very experienced lumber jack walking on a log! There are times such as this when I am rather grateful that he doesn't have sharp claws as I'm sure they would be digging in to secure his position.

He still will sneak up at any opportunity and gets quite insulted when I shift and force him to move. He will curse under his breath at me with irritated little whining growls and actually spread his arms to get a better hold. Some cats really have it tough......................

Cats sleep curled up in a tight little ball, right. Wrong! Nathan can get into more positions than a contortionist. I maintain that when he gets on the water bed, he actually paces off the footage of the bed so he can sleep in the dead centre all the time. It is absolutely amazing as he will sleep stretched out to his full extent, with his head turned up to the point that he is actually resting on the top of his head. His paws will be tucked in tightly to his little chest and his tail will be spread out like a gorgeous plume arched high over his back. It makes me feel uncomfortable just looking at him. He also likes to sleep on his back with his paws thrown out over his head.

Other times, I will find Nathan asleep with his head hanging well over the side of the bed, an arm stretched to its full extent in mid air and his body spread-eagled as if pressed into the bed by an iron. His favourite place to have a siesta is on kitchen chairs. I stipulate chairs, because he actually spans two chairs. These chairs ,of course, have nice padded cushions on them. His body is draped across one chair, while his head rests on the second chair. The fascinating part is that he allows his front legs (or arms as I call them) to hang down, totally relaxed. He wears a look that clearly says, "Don't bug me, I had a hard night". It would certainly indicate that he feels totally secure in his environment and no threats lurk on his horizon. But just to be on the safe side, his little ears are scoping like a radar for even the slightest sound.

As Nathan has matured, he also has developed his own individuality and shows great affection only to those he deems worthy and always on his terms. Hard to believe that he is the same fluff ball that I mistook for a rat so many years ago. He still maintains a slight wild side that keeps everyone guessing and thus provides him with that air of mystery that makes cats so special.

CHAPTER FOURTEEN

Mouse

It is a known fact that everyone should own a cat
named "Mouse". Once again, Sondra was on the trail of
finding a home for a cat. This seems to be a mission of which
she never tires and she always manages to find the most
unique felines. They are so special that I never can say
no to them joining our group of rogues.

Sondra has always had a great love of pure white cats
and on several occasions, brought home various pure white
cats. For some reason, they do not fair well and we always
end up losing them to rather tragic ends. As a result, I
became very reluctant to accept yet another white cat into
the family. Eventually, I agreed and have never regretted
the time that Mouse spent with me and how he enriched
my life.

One day while out for a drive, Sondra and her future
husband decided to stop by the local SPCA just to see what
furry little friends might be in need of a good home. In one
cage hiding under a pile of newspaper, they found a
bedraggled white Persian kitten, who appeared not to
respond to their voices at all. As white cats often have a
reduced hearing ability, they assumed that he was deaf, and
immediately, Sondra knew that she had to save him from

certain death as she rightly suspected that no one would want to care for a deaf animal.

There was only one problem, Sondra was still in school and had very little extra money. She would need to pay for his adoption, plus an additional fee to cover the cost of having him neutered at a later date. The neuter fee would be returned to her, but she required the money up front and time was running out on the kitten's stay at the SPCA. She was so upset when her fiancé, Jordan, left her at home that she went for a walk to think.

It was close to the end of the winter season and the snow was starting to melt. As she sat huddled on a park bench, her eye caught a glint of something shiny in the snow. When she went to investigate, she was amazed to discover a man's gold ring laying in the melting snow. She enquired with the local authorities and since no one had reported a lost ring, she was told that she could keep it. Here was the answer to her problem. She pawned the ring and was able to buy the little white kitten and save him from certain death. Obviously, it was meant to be.

She insisted that the kitten be retrieved at once and they were told that his name was "Mousse", which is the French word for a fluffy white pudding. A great name for a white cat, but Sondra's sense of humour took over and by Anglophying the name, he became "Mouse".

When they arrived home with him, we discovered that he had ear mites, a rather nasty problem, which can spread to the entire cat population. At this point, we already had three cats of various ages so poor Mouse was banished to Jordan's family business, where he became the office cat while the task of clearing up the ear mites was undertaken. Sondra faithfully made twice daily trips to the office to administer the ear drops, feed and care for him and spend time with him so that he knew he was loved and wanted. The entire family would drop in just to visit him and make him familiar with our scent.

While at the office, he became very pampered as the staff fell in love with him and took to bringing him various kitty toys. Before long, he had a basket full of special toys and kitty treats. The family would regularly receive updates on how Mouse looked as staff members would put him on the photocopier and take his photo. These photos were often rather distorted so I can only assume that being photocopied was not necessarily Mouse's favourite pastime.

Eventually the great day came when Mouse was finally free of ear mites and could join the feline population. There was only one problem. He had become a favourite of the office staff and they were more than a little reluctant to give him up. Once he joined our family, I clearly understood why he was so popular. This cat was and is personality personified. The best way to describe Mouse's personality is to say that without a doubt, he is the most laid-back cat I have ever met. Nothing ever bothers him. I always envision him as the type of gentlecat, who would lounge back in a deep soft easy chair, martini casually held in one paw as he just as casually held a cigarette aloof and asked if someone wouldn't mind just 'lighting him'! He simply loves life and everything in it. As a result, he had no problem being accepted by the local crowd and simply charmed his way into the feline circle.

Mouse loved to be around people and always greeted everyone who entered the house. There was a half wall that he loved to sit on and everyone who came in had to do a "high five" with Mouse. He actually held up his paw and waited for the person to give the sign back to him. He is a great ham and the kids would tell him to play "dead" at which point he would lay very still. Sondra maintained that he had no lips and after close inspection, I couldn't argue with her. As a result, his lower fangs hang down and can be easily seen, giving him a somewhat "vampire" quality and to rub his chin usually means connecting with these teeth. Somehow, it only adds to his charm as he manages to create an angelic look which offsets the sinister fangs.

CHAPTER FIFTEEN

Travels with Mouse

In order to transport Mouse, it was necessary to get him into a cage. Most cats absolutely hate to travel and the sight of the cage sends them into hiding. Once found, it is a major task to get them into the cage as they will claw and hang onto the sides of the box, biting , fighting and howling as if their very life depends on not getting inside that tiny room. Not so with Mouse. As soon as the cage comes out, it is essential that the door be left open, as he promptly moves in, sits very quietly and treats it just like an extension of the house. When ready to start a journey, one need only say, "In the box, Mouse," and he strolls in, gives a short meow and is all set to go.

Unlike most cats, Mouse loves to travel by car. Once on the move, Mouse likes to get out of the cage and is content to watch the world go by. One day, my son-in-law was returning from the city to the suburbs and had Mouse with him, quietly watching the other cars from his vantage point in the passenger's seat. It was rush hour traffic and the cars began to back up on a major bridge, eventually coming to a complete stand-still. Mouse chose this precise moment to decide that he had to use the litter box by looking up and giving a short meow. What does one do with a cat with a full bladder in rush hour traffic at a stand-still? Well, if the cat's name is Mouse, one simply opens the car door, holds the cat out, waits while he empties his bladder and meows to signal that he is finished, and returns him to his seat on the passenger side!!!!!!!!!!

Shortly after Mouse joined the family, the young ones decided to move to another city across the country and we were all sad to see them move so far away and knew that Mouse would be greatly missed, too. The journey was to be made by car and would take several days. They planned to stay at motels enroute, which created something of a problem as not all establishments welcomed pets and they certainly were not going to leave Mouse in the car overnight, by himself. Sondra thought about it as they travelled and came to the conclusion that they would simply smuggle him into the room for the night. She had taken a pillow along in the car and decided to remove the pillow case, which would serve as a bag. When the time came to get Mouse from the car to the room, she simply opened the bag, told Mouse to climb in, put the bag over her shoulder, and strolled through the lobby and up to the room. I can't imagine another cat being so obliging.

Some years later, the young people decided to move to California, and because Mouse could not travel by air because of a heart condition, we agreed to make the trip by car and deliver Mouse to his new home. He is a delight to travel with as he really loves the car. He is invited into the box and settles down quite happily until out on the highway. Then the door is propped open and he has free run of the car. He loves to sit in the front seat and put his paws up on the dash. Thus arranged, he proceeds to watch the scenery go by. If someone is occupying the front seat, this is not a problem as he simply sits on any available lap. He also likes to perch on top of the box for a while and eventually drape himself across the back window and sleeps.

On this particular trip, I was wearing a shirt that had rather heavy shoulder pads and he decided he quite liked laying across the back of the front seat between my head and the head rest. This didn't create any difficulty for me as I am rather short and there was plenty of room for him to stretch out. As the day progressed, I took my turn at driving and Mouse felt he would like to continue to perch on the back of the seat. We started off, Mouse was allowed out of the cage and proceeded to make his way back to his perch. The only problem was that now Les occupied that seat and alas, he wasn't equipped with shoulder pads. As Mouse balanced himself, he extended his claws for support and sunk them into an unprotected shoulder! A bellow erupted, the cat beat a hasty retreat and spent the remainder of the day watching the world from a safe distance in the back seat. A rather wise decision on his part, I felt!

We also discovered that Mouse really likes to help drive the car and if allowed, will sit on the driver's lap and place his paws on the steering wheel. I always think that he would look very dapper wearing a sporty racing cap with a pipe in the corner of his lipless mouth. He is such a distinguished looking gent with his lovely pure white coat.

As we travelled further south and the temperature became increasingly warmer, Mouse was less active and as we travelled across the desert, he very sensibly took refuge in the lowest part of the car, refusing any food or water. He lay on the floor of the car and remained as still as possible. His body also began to shed fur and before long, it looked as if it was snowing cat fur inside the car, which naturally had a dark fabric upholstery. As we neared the ocean, we didn't need a map to tell us. Mouse became more active and took a renewed interest in the trip again. He must have smelt the sea air and cooler temperatures hours before we did. Upon arriving at Sondra and Jordan's home, there was a great reunion of all concerned and Mouse was left to explore his new home.

Sondra spent the next hour getting all of Mouse's excess fur out of the car and the following day, Mouse appeared to have lost about four pounds as he literally dropped a bag full of fur within the first 24 hours in the warmer climate. It had always amazed me just how adaptable cats are and if they feel secure, they settle in very quickly to any new surroundings.

CHAPTER SIXTEEN

Kiss

When the young ones first moved so far from home, Mouse was very lonely at their new home as he was left alone all day. He was accustomed to having an entire pride of cats to keep him company, so it was decided that Mouse needed a companion. One day, Jordan arrived home and told Sondra to choose a pocket which held a surprise. Inside the pocket, she found the tiniest kitten all curled up. The kitten was so tiny that she sat in the palm of Sondra's hand. It should be mentioned here that by this time, Mouse had reached his full adult size of about 16 pounds and looked even larger because of his fur coat. Since the kitten was a gift, she was soon named "Kiss". For quite a period of time, Kiss thought Jordan was her 'mommy' and was happiest when she could curl as close to him as possible.

It was love at first sight for Mouse and he adopted Kiss as his little sister to be protected from everything. She needs only to squeak and he is on the dead run to rescue and protect her. Because of his nature, Mouse is the perfect companion for Kiss as she is the ultimate fuss budget cat. Kiss has never grown to any size and is so tiny that she has earned the nickname of "Itty Bitty Buddy" by Les, who thinks she is a little princess. Not everyone would agree with that description as she is forever complaining about something in a wispy little voice. When Mouse gets fed up with her nonsense, he simply sits on top of her and all that can be heard are pathetic little muffled protests as she struggles to free herself.

Jordan had a lovely black sports car that was his pride and joy. As Mouse was an excellent traveller, he was allowed free roam of the car at all times; therefore, Jordan was somewhat unprepared for the incident involving Kiss. When Kiss was still very young, it was necessary to take her out in the car and without thinking, Jordan opened the box to allow Mouse access to the car. Too late, Jordan realised just how much Kiss hated the car as she scurried out of the box and promptly christened the lovely interior of the sports car. That was the first and only time that she was ever allowed out of the box in the car!

It really isn't a great idea to ever run out of cat food and the problem is only compounded if there just happens to be two cats who really hate to miss a meal. However, sometimes it happens in the best of organised households. Sondra discovered on her way out to work one day that they were, indeed, out of food. Arriving home from work late that night and rather tired, she dropped a large bag of cat food on the kitchen floor intending to feed the cats, but got interrupted. She went off to bed without feeding the hungry beasties. The following morning, the kitten was missing and it was only after searching the entire apartment that they went to check the bag of cat food. The bag had been ripped open and Kiss was fast asleep on top of the food with a bulging belly. Mouse was found curled up around a huge potted plant and by the amount of food missing from the bag, they concluded that the cats must have had a feast to end all feasts.

CHAPTER SEVENTEEN

On the Move Again

By this time, we had joined the children in the new area and saw a good deal of their cats. On occasion, the cats would come to stay during holiday times and it was always great to have them around, even if it did swell the ranks of the cat population to five. The house is very large and there is plenty of room for everyone, especially as they all co-habited well together. Having got so attached to the young cats, it was sad news when Sondra told us they were moving to the U.S. permanently. Nevertheless I was determined to make the move as easy as possible for the children and the cats.

The cats required complete medical documentation to move to another country so appointments were made. Because of job commitments, Christopher was tasked to take the cats for their examinations and shots. They have to travel in the same carry cage so out came the box and a very willing Mouse was all set for the trip. Not quite the case with Kiss. She hates the box and any kind of car travel. Mouse ambles into the box and then the serious business starts of getting Kiss in the box. It would best be accomplished with a crowbar! To put Kiss in first is the worst possible idea as Mouse takes his own sweet time to stroll into the box, by which time Kiss is long gone and good luck in catching her. In the end, Christopher got a very willing Mouse all set and literally rammed Kiss in and slammed the door shut. Off they went to see the vet.

Kiss was given a clean bill of health and the mountain of paper work processed. Upon examining the big guy, the vet detected a problem with his heart. As Mouse is not an old gent, this was a little surprising and the vet wanted to double check. Another appointment was made for Mouse and in due course, he was taken for a follow-up. This was really amazing as he was hooked up to the heart monitor and the monitor was slaved into a long distance link-up in Chicago, where feline heart specialists took the readings. After the test was completed, the specialist came on the line and asked what trick the vet was playing. The vet assured him that there was no trick and that a real cat was ,indeed, hooked up to the system. There was a request for a second reading and the specialist was amazed that the cat could actually be alive as he had an extensive heart defect, which could only be attributed to a birth defect. I can only conclude that Mouse is a survivor and his personality is such that he never gets upset or over-excited so no stress is put on that wonderful heart of his.

The only problem that was created was that Mouse was not able to travel by air and since that was the way he was to be transported to California, we had to come up with an alternative plan. Since we had planned to visit the children shortly, we agreed to take Mouse by car, in a couple of months. This suited me just fine as I would be able to enjoy Mouse, (whom I considered to be my 'grandcat') for a period of time and I knew he loved to travel by car.

Itty Bitty Buddy was airlifted when Christopher took a short holiday to visit his sister. I'm told that the trip to the airport with Kiss in the cage, alone, was a nightmare of temper tantrum at being separated for the only time in her life from her big brother, plus that fact that she hated the car and cage. The cage is carpeted and she actually attempted to lift the carpet and climb under it. She howled and clawed the walls in sheer fury and, in general, made the trip as unpleasant as she possibly could for everyone. She only settled down when she had arrived safely at her new home and was welcomed with great delight by Sondra, who hadn't seen her for three months.

Moving the cats to a much warmer climate created another set of problems which the kids were not aware of initially. Any number of insects thrive in the hot climate and as summer progressed, both Mouse and Kiss started to scratch a great deal. It didn't take long to figure out that they had acquired some livestock in the form of fleas and since no one was interested in starting a flea circus, they had to be eliminated quickly.

A visit to the pet shop provided the necessary flea shampoo and then the fun began. Mouse was quite content to enjoy the bath and took it all in stride. Not so with Kiss, which was no surprise to anyone. Sondra first armed herself by dressing in heavy weight denim jeans, a long sleeved shirt and sneakers. They then filled the tub, Sondra got in and the ordeal began. Kiss tried to climb the shower curtain, the walls, Sondra's body as if it were the trunk of a tree and eventually the porcelain tub! The scary part was that the baths had to be done a number of times during the hot weather and it became a test of wills to see who outlasted whom. The cooler fall weather was reason to celebrate for humans and cats alike.

The fascinating part of the bath scenario is that as much as Kiss hates to have the very necessary flea decontamination baths, she loves to get her tail wet. Now, it can only be the tip of her tail that is dipped in water and then she will happily suck on it as if it was a soother. She starts by licking her tail much like a dog, until it is groomed just to her satisfaction, which can take some considerable time. Eventually, contented little sharp purrs will start to emit from her and then she will settle into a full blown, out and out, purr, sucking until she drifts off to sleep, usually curled tightly against Mouse.

CHAPTER EIGHTEEN

Mouse and Kiss Anecdotes

Mouse and Kiss both love the Christmas tree as do most cats. It is a wonderful place to play with all the ornaments and tinsel. However, Mouse takes it a step further, as he feels that all those pretty trinkets were put there just for his pleasure and the entire holiday season is spent re-decorating the tree as he systematically undecorated various parts of it. If he is particularly fond of something, it will find its way off the tree a number of times during the holidays. He has to be constantly reminded that it isn't a particularly good idea to chew on the wiring for the lights, especially when the power is turned on!!

Mouse had always loved to sleep in the bathroom sink and since he was acclimatising to the warmer climate, he really enjoyed the large sink in the new house as it was lovely and cool. Sondra often gets up in the night and rather than turn on lights, simply makes her way to the bathroom in the dark. Not knowing that Mouse had taken up residence in the sink, she groped for a water glass and not being able to lay hands on one, decided to drink right from the tap. As she bent over, mouth open for a drink, she was both startled and disgusted to receive a mouth full of fur instead of the expected cold water. It hasn't stopped Mouse from sleeping in the sink, but everyone knows to check it first before turning on the tap in the dark.

Mouse has developed a somewhat unique problem of

recent as he actually appears to be outgrowing his cat suit. He has put on a considerable amount of weight and one can actually see his lovely pink belly when he rolls over. Because he is so white and his skin is a gorgeous pink colour, it is even more pronounced. The big decision seems to be whether to put him on a diet, which isn't likely or get him turned on to doing some catarobics. The jury is still out on deciding which is the better choice and in the meantime, his suit gets smaller and smaller.

Being on the portly side has been a problem that has plagued Mouse for a period of time. Having finished dinner one evening while watching television, the kids were relaxing and the dinner plates still lay on the coffee table, which had a wood finish. Mouse obviously felt that the plates had been left for his inspection and he took a mighty leap onto the coffee table. Unfortunately, he misjudged the height and distance, lost his centre of gravity and started to slide off the edge of the table. Sadly, his front claws had sunk into the wood, held fast and left him stranded, half on and half off the table with the most pathetic look on his face. He was diagnosed by Jordan as being spastic and after suffering the humiliation of being lifted back up so he could retract his claws and thus free himself, he took himself off to parts unknown to restore his shattered pride.

When Kiss was about six months old, she started to attack feet. Any foot was fair game for her, but she also had incredibly sharp little claws and teeth. It began with attacks on feet under bed covers, which protected the feet from the lethal claws; however, it soon progressed to more devious assaults on unsuspecting humans, so Jordan decided it was time to cure her, once and for all. He got into bed and casually dangled his foot over the side. Kiss saw it immediately and took a great leap at the foot. At that precise moment, he pulled his foot away and Kiss hung as if suspended in mid-air for a matter of seconds before crashing to the floor in a heap. That definitely cured her and put an end to her vicious attacks.

Kiss has a passion for bugs. Large or small ones, make

no difference to her, as long as they crawl, Kiss will stalk them on tiny cat paws. She will remain completely motionless for several minutes as she watches an unsuspecting bug making its way across the room. Then, with lightening quick speed, she gathers all of her strength into her back haunches and leaps forward. The bug never knows what hit it and she then proceeds to daintily devour the morsel. Sondra always tells Kiss that "you are what you eat". As Kiss continues to eat bugs, one can only conclude that she is totally unconcerned with that assessment. Her best hunting talent is to catch airborne bugs in mid flight and have them consumed before she hits the floor. One can only assume that she considers them as extra protein.

When the family lived on the flight path of a major airport, the cats spend a good deal of time sitting in the window watching the various aircraft coming in the land. The planes were on final descend so came very low over the buildings and Kiss watched them with such keen interest that I often wondered if she was judging distance and altitude in an attempt to snag the biggest bug she had ever seen!

Mouse has conned Kiss on many occasions as he will quietly walk into the room, sit down and stare at the wall. Before long, Kiss will join him and frantically search the entire wall area, looking for that elusive bug. Even humans have been tricked by his ploy and I have found myself following his eyes as I attempt to locate what it is that has caught his attention. He must be silently laughing at all of us as he will get up, take one backward glance and wander off, leaving one with the uneasy feeling that perhaps maybe the eyes are starting to fail just a bit. Kiss still hasn't caught on to his private joke and will continue to gaze longingly at the wall in hopes that a multi-legged little bug will appear for her enjoyment.

Kiss is also fascinated by birds. Not that she has ever actually had contact with one or would know what to do if she did catch one. She does like to sit in the window and watch all the feathered little creatures as they swoop down and land on the bushes and tree branches near her. She will watch them intently and then crouch down as if stalking them. She then makes the most fascinating sound that is very similar to a rapid action machine gun being fired. The birds seem rather unmoved by this threat, but she continues none the less and dreams of the day when she can actually remove that strip of screening that separates her from her prey.

Paper is a delight for most cats and Mouse is especially fond of any kind of paper. He will wait expectantly as an item is unwrapped and then sit poised for the paper to be wadded into a ball and thrown for him. If the mood moves him, he will gallop off after the paper, pick it up carefully with his teeth and retrieve it for the person. This does take some time, though as he will only do it if he's in the right frame of mind; otherwise, he will watch as the paper is wadded up, poise himself as if ready to chase it and then watch the ball land on the far side of the room. He will then look at the person with his big brown eyes and one can almost hear him thinking, "If you think I'm going to chase and retrieve that stupid thing, you've been hanging around dogs again"!

Mouse also is quite fond of the plastic used to seal milk lids and is always delighted to see a new container of milk being opened. He sits expectantly as the plastic is peeled off and then he is given his toy which he will play with for hours. Once he loses interest, he will discard it for the present only to return to play with it until all that is left is a chewed, mangled mess. This does give him the much needed exercise that he requires, but sometimes it is a little annoying to hear him chasing around the house in the wee hours of the morning and tackling Kiss if she attempts to take it away from him. I'm never certain which is worst, the noise made from chasing after the ridiculous piece of plastic or the dispute over who gets to play with it. Either way, it ensures lost sleep and the only way to settle the matter is to take the plastic away from both of them, give them a scolding and order them off to bed. Whoever said having a family of cats was a soothing experience has never lived with the crowd that we share dwellings with.

Mouse became very fond of ladies handbags recently and would investigate any bags left open on the floor or table. Should there be something of particular interest to him, he simply proceeded to climb right inside the handbag and have a good snoop. Sondra told him to kindly only retrieve twenty dollar bills or higher and/or any gold credit cards. They are still working on perfecting this as Mouse really is just curious as to what ladies really carry in those enormous handbags. A question that has indeed plagued men for many years!

Because of the distance, I didn't get to see the grand cats as often as I would like, but it was always a treat to make the trip as they would be waiting at the door to greet me warmly. They always seemed to remember who I was and made to feel most welcome as they would curl up to sleep with me whenever I visited. Kiss even mellowed with age and came to sleep on my lap as I sat reading or visiting with Sondra. They have always been delightful companions and I enjoyed the time shared with them.

CHAPTER NINETEEN

They're Back

Two years passed and I had made several delightful trips to Southern California to visit with the children and grandcats. The cats seemed to have settled into the warmer climate and although I often noticed several bites on their skin, they seemed unconcerned by the situation. Therefore, I was rather alarmed when I received a phone call one Sunday from Jordan asking if I would consider giving the cats a home in Canada again. We talked at length and I agreed to fly down to California as soon as possible. In the meantime, he would take care of getting them to the vet for medical exams and shots to obtain the necessary documentation in order to clear the animals to leave the U.S. and re-enter Canada.

I was totally unprepared for the scene that greeted me when I arrived at the apartment. Mouse was his usual "Mr. Congeniality" and ran to welcome me with delighted little sounds and his tail held high. My first impression was that Mouse had lost some weight, but then he turned around and I was shocked to realise that he had almost no fur from his shoulders on back and his hind legs, tail and belly were completely bald, save for the very tip of his tail. There were little tufts of fur on his back paws, which gave his the look of a poodle who had just been given a fancy clip. On close inspection, his back was covered with bites and open sores where he had been chewing at the bites.

Kiss came to greet me as well, but rather timidly. I noticed that she had also lost some of her coat in the flank area and a section of her tail. When I picked her up to check on her more closely, I discovered that her little pink belly was completely bald as well and she also had several bites and sores although not as severe as poor Mouse. Both cats seemed obsessed with scratching and licking their coats or what was left of them.

The vet had diagnosed that both cats had developed some sort of an allergy to plants that grow in California, which I found odd as they had been in the environment for over two years by this time. My own assessment was that they had been overrun by fleas, however, I was more concerned with getting the "babies" back to Canada where I could get them proper care. Our immediate concern was that Mouse was not able to be airlifted because of his heart condition. I mentioned this and was assured that the vet could find no defect when she examined Mouse. She had also hooked him up to the heart monitor and got very distorted readings, but concluded that because he loves to be held, that what was affecting the readings was his wonderful deep throaty purring. Needless to say, I had rather grave misgivings about her diagnosis. She certified his fit for air travel and because of the deteriorating condition of both cats, I was most anxious to get them out of their present situation.

I had arrived with tranquillisers for travelling so proceeded to make the travel plans. I had to drive from San Diego to Los Angeles by car with the cats in one carry cage as they always travel better together. I had certain misgivings about the trip as I had to go through morning rush hour traffic on the freeway and Kiss is a lousy companion in the car. Sondra and I administered the pills to them, waited a little while for the pills to take effect and then put the cats in the cage.

Off I went into the teeth of morning traffic braced for the worst from both the road and the cats. The traffic was all I had anticipated with several car accidents, flashing police lights and delays...just the average traffic flow of Southern California.

I anxiously kept checking the cats in the cage on the

seat beside me, whenever I dared to take my eyes off the road and they seemed content as the car moved along. Only once did Kiss begin to fuss when I had to stop in congested traffic and I was treated to a very touching scene. As Kiss started to cry, Mouse gently reached over and cupped her tiny body in his large paw, drawing her in closely against his body, licked her cheek to reassure her and they both settled into a tranquil sleep.

Once at L.A.X., I turned in the rental car and was amazed at all the attention travelling with two cats can generate. So many people wanted to know what was in the box, and upon learning there were two cats inside, wanted to see and touch them. Ever the curious gent, Mouse wanted to say "hello" to all, while Kiss hide in the furthest most corner of the box. I had many welling hands to assist in transporting them. I continued to be very nervous about Mouse's ability to survive a three hour flight so found a quiet place to prepare him for the journey and get them away from curious onlookers. They had to be loaded in a separate area and I loathed leaving them even for a short time for although I had airlifted cats on occasion before, I had never done so with cats in less than perfect health and this really worried me.

I went to the gate for the flight as it was announced and as they started to board the plane, I suddenly got an eerie feeling that I had to check about my cats. My ticket indicated that they were travelling with me so went to the counter and asked for confirmation that the cats had, indeed, been placed on board already. A call to the ground crew was all that was needed, but no one seemed to be able to find them! Instant panic!!!!! I refused to board the plane until they had been located as it was the last plane leaving for Canada that day and I was not about to leave them behind. Frantic phone calls continued as I was encouraged to at least board the plane while the search continued.

Reluctantly, I went to the plane, but refused to take my seat while the crew continued to try and locate the missing cats. I was about to leave the aircraft when the flight attendant came rushing up to me with a big smile. Not only had the "babies" been located, but they were safely on board in the pressurised cargo bay and letting everyone know that they were very much alive. Now my only worry was that Mouse would make it home.

I left California's tropical climate to arrive home in a snow storm in April. Not all that uncommon for us, but what a shock it must have been for two cats who had spent two years in a hot climate and were arriving minus their furry little coats. I was in a rush to clear customs and immigration so that I could find them and make sure that Mouse was all right. The cage was waiting for me as I arrived and two little faces were pressed against the wire mess looking for me. I was so relieved to see them both safe and alive that I sat down on the floor in the middle of the luggage area and opened the cage to check them out. I sent up a little prayer of thanks when I was greeted with little soft purrs and nudges as if to reassure me that all was well. The next stop was Agriculture Department clearance, after which the entire cage was wrapped in a huge blanket and transported to the heated car and we were finally headed for home, safe and sound.

I had definite mixed feelings about being home as I knew the first thing I had to do was keep Mouse and Kiss separated from my three cats until I could get them into flea baths so we didn't have an epidemic on our hands. I anticipated that the shock of an icy Canadian snow storm would have taken its toll on the majority of any fleas brave enough to make the journey, but I couldn't take any chances. These poor animals had already endured so much, but I knew this was for their own good and it would be easier to have the bath done with while they were still under the effects of the pills they had received earlier in the day.

I'm sure they must have wondered what they had done to deserve such treatment. First to be taken from their home and people, pills shoved down their throats, crammed in a box, taken on a road trip, lost and found in an airport, flown in a plane and then another car trip only to be met at the end of it with a flea bath, all before even getting a drink, food or a chance to use the litter box!!!!!!!!!!!!!! At any rate, the flea baths were accomplished with only minor shredding of the hands and both cats were rolled into huge bath towels and rubbed down. Then they were free to get re-acquainted with the relatives.

Because both cats had lived in the house prior to their travels, they were familiar with the surroundings and the other cats. Almost immediately, Mouse discovered a stuffed mouse that was his favourite toy and had a wonderful time getting to know it all over again. They found the food, water and litter boxes all in the same place and returned to using their favourite sleeping places as if they had never left.

One more trip was necessary and this time it was to see our family vet, whom I trust totally ever since he saved Minkey's life. He confirmed that Mouse and Kiss had indeed been subjected to a massive infestation of fleas and although we had been successful in eradicating the fleas, there were massive bites that needed to be cared for. So began a prolonged term of medication and it reached the point where both cats would disappear when I walked into the room as they knew I was about to shove more pills down their throats. Along with it came yet another round of flea baths, just to be on the safe side and I think we were all very happy to see the end of the baths and the medication. Slowly, the fur began to reappear. Kiss recovered her coat much faster as she had far less to grow back, but poor Mouse took three weeks before I began to even notice any significant changes. No doubt the other cats didn't help his ego as one could almost hear them laughing behind their paws whenever he walked across the room as they all turned to watch him pass. I'm sure that only his good nature saw him through this crisis.

So the cat family was complete again and I knew I had done the right thing when I walked into the bedroom one day about a month after our eventful journey and found all five cats asleep on the water bed!

CHAPTER TWENTY

Tail Ends

Brandy was an enormous ginger coloured cat. He also was an incredible hunter. The house was situated in an almost rural environment, so he had lots of room to roam the fields and ditches. At first, I found it quite interesting when he would arrive home with the occasional morsel that he had hunted down. He would arrive at the front door with the sad remains of a rodent and I would tell him what a magnificent hunter he was. Unfortunately, he took my praise as a sign that he should catch more. Before long, Brandy was bringing home more and more carcasses for my approval.

Eventually, it became a daily event to find six dead rats neatly lined up on the front porch and they came to be known as Brandy's daily six pack. I refused to clear them away so every night when Les arrived home from work, he would get the shovel and plastic bag to dispose of the daily catch. One day, I looked out the window and watched in horror as Brandy dragged a dead rat home, the rat being almost as big as the cat! It was impossible to break him of the habit of retrieving and I suffered through many six packs while Brandy was with us.

Brandy loved to be with people and when the weather was nice, I enjoyed going for a daily walk. I never had to go alone as Brandy would follow me, always walking along the narrow cement curbing. Often, I would take along a bag of knitting and stop in for a visit with my friend who lived about a block away. Brandy especially liked to visit as he knew that meant there would be treats for him. When the door opened and we were invited in, Brandy would run into the kitchen, position himself in front of the microwave and patiently wait as Jeanette filled a bowl with milk and warmed it for him in the microwave. The minute the unit stopped, he would pace back and forth until the bowl was set on a place mat kept just for him and he would daintily lap up the warm milk. Once finished, he demanded to go outdoors to inspect the yard. When my visit was finished, Brandy would be waiting for me in the front yard. We would start off home and after about ten feet, he would begin to complain loudly. At this point, I would open the knitting bag and he would jump in and get a ride back home.

For all his hunting ability, Brandy was a delightful gent and was extremely affectionate. He adorned Christopher and they always slept together. Therefore, it was a sad day when Brandy went missing. The children combed the fields and ditches fearing that he had been hit by a car and was left to suffer. We called the local authorities, who couldn't help, and even asked all through the neighbourhood in hopes that someone would be able to give us a clue as to his disappearance.

The following week, a letter appeared in the local paper from a very irate citizen who had nearly had her cat snatched from her front step. She had gone to the authorities to investigate and discovered that the city had hired a rather unsavoury character to catch whatever cats he found roaming around and he was selling them to a research establishment who paid him handsomely . Not only that, but the city was paying him to engage in this despicable practise. He had decided to make every cat his prey. The lady wanted to make all pet owners aware and had even described the blue van that cruised the streets·day and night.

When I mentioned it to my neighbours, they were horrified as the husband had been awakened in the middle of the night the previous week by a noise and upon investigating, found someone near his car. He had scared the person off, but noted that they drove a blue van. We realised that it was the same time that Brandy had disappeared. A frantic call confirmed our worst fears and we mourned the passing of our great hunter.

Not content to leave it at that, we then wrote letters to the city council and mayor, deploring their attitude anddemanded that action be taken to stop further cat snatching. That ended the reign of terror by the blue van, but couldn't return our much loved Brandy.

Grey was another gent who joined us for a brief time. One day, the local group was lounging on the deck in the sun and I went out to give them a treat. I was a little startled to find an extra feline gazing up at me. This was most unusual, as the cats were very territorial and allowed no cats in the yard. He was a magnificent Russian Blue. These cats are a charcoal grey colour, with enormous green eyes and the most luscious double thick fur coat. He obviously was lost so I picked him up and examined him for a tattoo. Just as I suspected, he had his mark in the ear and I went to make some phone calls, soon coming up with a name. Imagine my surprise when the people claimed they hadn't lost their pet as he stood big as life on my deck. I could only conclude that they didn't want him, so he was invited to join us.

For lack of a better name, we took to calling him Grey Cat which was shortened to Grey. He loved to get attention and came and went as he pleased, always ready when the food bowls were being filled. I soon discovered that he couldn't stay in the house for long periods of time as his coat was so thick that he would overheat. Periodically, he would disappear for a few days so we took to calling him the wandering cat. Eventually, the periods of absence became greater until he was gone totally. Several months later, he stopped by, just to say hello and get something to eat before he left again. I have come to the conclusion that some cats are not meant to be domesticated and chose to be masters of their own destiny.

Herman was a great cat, pure white and had some

interesting habits. This cat loved food and wasn't content to just accept the cat food that was provided. He discovered early on that the humans in the family got their food from the fridge and that was the place to be. He took to sleeping in front of the fridge with his nose almost touching the door and whenever the door was opened and he was compelled to move, he promptly made every attempt to climb right inside to see what goodies he could eat. I learned very quickly to always check before closing the door.

He also liked to be entertained in a rather odd sort of a way. He would wonder into the family room and arrange himself in front of the television set, where he would quietly sit for hours. There was only one problem. Should anyone happen to come in and turn ON the set, he promptly got up and left. No one ever did figure our exactly what it was that he saw on the screen when the set was turned off, and frankly, no one really wanted to find out!

When Herman was a kitten, he showed me what the meaning of taking a cat nap really meant. He would be walking across the floor, hit a patch of sunshine and do a somewhat undignified nose dive. He would be asleep instantly with his little nose pressed into the carpet. There he would sleep for several hours, at which point he would awake, stretch and proceed on his way as if nothing had happened.

Harley lived with a very close friend of mine. Harley was a wimpy little cat who ran and hid whenever someone arrived at the door. He was, however, very social with the family and especially looked forward to the time of day when the family arrived home as they always had a cocktail before dinner. As soon as Harley heard the clink of bottle and glass, he would fly into the kitchen, up on the counter and then to the top of the fridge, where he sat watching the cocktails being prepared. Three glasses were set out and into the third glass went an extra olive and a splash of olive juice. Cocktails prepared, Harley joined the family in the lounge as they all enjoyed their refreshments and Harley was allowed at this time to perch on the coffee table as he savoured his cocktail and extra olive!

Harley's family lived in a rather secluded area, so decided it would be a good idea to have a rather sophisticated alarm system installed as only Harley and an aged deaf dog were home during the day. The system was a laser alarm which criss-crossed the room at various levels. This was state of the art technology, but they hadn't reckoned with a cat. The alarm was activated late the first night and before long, it was triggered. The authorities responded and a very embarrassed friend said it was a false alarm. Unfortunately, the alarm continued to be activated so the alarm company was called to investigate. Only then did they discover that when no one was around, Harley literally strutted his stuff and pranced around with his tail held straight over his head, causing the laser to be activated as the tip of his tail skimmed the beam. A very shy and upset Harley was held and his tail measured to its full extent plus half an inch and all beams were reset. That ended the false alarms.

A friend of mine owes a lovely little lady Manx cat. Manx are a rather unusual breed and are not very plentiful. The feline came into "heat" and sent several messages to her people that she was looking for a gentleman so my friend tried repeatedly to find a suitable Manx gent and was nearly at her wit's end. One evening, the cat manages to slip out the door and was gone.

Heartsick, my friend thought that she had seen her beloved cat for the last time as the cat never went outdoors. Imagine her shock a week later when the Manx suddenly appeared at the door and demanded to be let in. As the cat sauntered in, totally unconcerned, the friend stood in stunned silence as a very elegant gentleman Manx followed the young lady into the house. The female looked up at her human as if to say, "Since you couldn't find me a mate, I went out and found my own". The gent moved in and has never left!

These, then, are the cat tales. For every cat, there is a unique story, for cats are themselves so unique!

The "Cat Tails" Cats
From left to right: Minkey, Chuck, Nathan, Mouse, Miss Kiss.